Slayers

VOL. 5: THE SILVER BEAST

WRITTEN BY
HAJIME KANZAKA

ILLUSTRATED BY
RUI ARAIZUMI

TOKYOPOP®

HAMBURG // LONDON // LOS ANGELES // TOKYO

Slayers Vol. 5: The Silver Beast
Written by Hajime Kanzaka
Illustrated by Rui Araizumi

Translation - Jeremiah Bourque
English Adaptation - Jay Antani
Associate Editor - Lianne Sentar
Copy Editor - Abigail Phillips
Proofreader - Suzanne Waldman
Design and Layout - Jose Macasocol, Jr.
Cover Design - Jorge Negrete

Editor - Nicole Monastirsky
Digital Imaging Manager - Chris Buford
Production Managers - Jennifer Miller and Mutsumi Miyazaki
Managing Editor - Jill Freshney
VP of Production - Ron Klamert
Publisher and E.I.C. - Mike Kiley
President and C.O.O. - John Parker
C.E.O. - Stuart Levy

A  Novel

TOKYOPOP Inc.
5900 Wilshire Blvd. Suite 2000
Los Angeles, CA 90036

E-mail: info@TOKYOPOP.com
Come visit us online at www.TOKYOPOP.com

ISBN: 978-1-59532-581-5

First TOKYOPOP printing: September 2005
10 9 8 7 6 5 4 3 2
Printed in Canada

CONTENTS

1: THE PROBLEM WITH A CULT FOLLOWING

The barrage of clichés dropped down on us like monkey poop.

"Hand over the coin if you value your lives," snarled the masked bandit.

One of the other rogues, who probably realized we weren't taking his gang very seriously, brandished his long sword at us. But that only made him look lamer.

Someone's obviously overcompensating.

I think the three of us—Gourry, Amelia, and I—all yawned simultaneously.

"W-what?!" grunted the first bandit. "What's with the attitude here?! Don't get smart!"

Why would I need *smarts* around a bunch of bozos?

"It's not being smart," I told him in a glum tone. "It's just resignation." I sighed, casting a glance at the dirt path below my feet.

"Man," I grumbled, "I thought nobody used these back roads anymore. But no, we get one idiotic bandit gang after another. I can't get any peace, can I?"

I decided to lay it on pretty thick and get the guy riled up. "We'd all be better off if you back-road bandits grew some balls and did your business out on the main road where the real action is. Y'know, like real highway robbers. But maybe you're too chicken to die like real men."

The bandits stared at us slack-jawed, probably too stunned to believe what they heard. Stretching my arms, I went on.

"Ever since we started on this road, you're the . . . I dunno, third group of bandits to hold us up today? You understand why I lose track of these things."

"H-hey, hey, hey!" the bandit protested. "Wait a sec. You're not gonna pull the old 'The Bandits up the Road Took Everything So We've Got Nothing to Give You' routine, are ya?!"

I rolled my eyes. *This guy just doesn't get it, does he?*

"It's *annoying* having to beat up riff-raff like you all day," I snapped. "Gimme a break, okay?"

"Annoying?" piped in Gourry from my side. "I dunno. The last bunch of guys seemed pretty shrewd to me."

Ah, Gourry—one of my traveling companions, the slightly clueless comic relief. He's your typical tall, blond, and handsome hero type. And did I mention he's an ultra kick-ass swordsman? Maybe the best I've ever seen. Unfortunately, he also has the brains of a crab.

"Shut up!" I grunted from the corner of my mouth. "They were nothing but trash! And I'm busy here."

Tormenting bandits. It's one of my favorite pastimes.

It can give you a hell of a rush, y'see—ambushing a large group of crooks and pummeling the crap out of them, then, when they're dead and you've wiped the dust off your clothes, you sort through their stolen loot and take what you like. Plundering from evil plunderers; no harm in that. And so what if I'm a little greedy? It's my guilty pleasure. My craving for treasure is what gets me up in the morning.

Not only that, but this little hobby allows me, warrior and sorceress Lina Inverse, to keep my fighting and magic skills in tip-top shape. Your average warrior sorceress attacked by bandits for ten days straight would have most certainly been on a one-way trip to the afterlife, but for me, it had served as a decent workout. Maybe bandits always resort to cheesy lines and tend to stink, but squaring off with them can be somewhat interesting because of their clever use of surrounding terrain.

Lately, though, all of them had the same effect on me: flat-out boredom. So I waited to see what sort of spin our new bunch of dorks would put on a tired, old act.

"Okay," I said. "So you guys have gotta have some serious loot on you, right? Y'know, to make this worth it."

"C-can it!" the bandit stuttered. "You've got some nerve considering you're at our mercy, little girl!"

Little girl? And since when am I at anyone's mercy?

"Fine!" the bandit roared. "So you wanna fight it out, do ya?!"

"Sheesh," I moaned, truly bored. I slipped off my mantle and let it fall with a dull thud; I saw Gourry extend his hand toward the hilt of his sword.

"Hey," muttered another of the masked bandits, almost as an afterthought. "What the hell is *that*?"

"What's what?" asked the first bandit. His friend pointed at the silhouetted figure of my other companion, Amelia, who now stood in a nearby tree.

"That looks like . . . someone standing in a tree," commented the first bandit, sounding surprised and confused.

"Thank you, Captain Obvious."

"Who've you got up there?" the bandit snapped.

"Just give it a sec," I answered shortly. "And we're not done with this conversation."

"Uh . . . if you say so," the bandit replied slowly. "A-anyway, I say we drop the small talk and settle things by force!"

He was about to make a move when Amelia boomed out from the trees.

"That's far enough, villains!" she roared, her voice resounding like the Voice of Doom.

"What?!" shouted the first bandit.

"Where?!" another hollered.

The bandits huddled in a group, darting panicky glances all over the place.

It was the sort of stupidity you read about in storybooks. One of them shouted and pointed to the tree their fearless leader had mentioned thirty seconds earlier, and the lot of them—*including* the leader—gasped in surprise.

This is all kinds of sad.

In the tree, of course, was Amelia, now a single step into the sunlight and no longer hidden by the leaves' shadows. She stood proudly on her branch like some all-powerful deity about to rain hellfire on the rest of us.

As it turned out, Amelia was about to rain down something much worse: a speech.

"Wherever there is death, there is life," Amelia announced. "Wherever there is darkness, there is light. Wherever there is evil, there is justice! You have lost your way and surrendered your souls to the blackness that is immorality!"

Then, like the drama queen she is, she raised her arm and pointed a condemning finger at the bandits. "As heaven's executioner, I shall mete out your punishment under the blazing sun! No matter what excuses you offer, know you can no longer escape your fate!"

In simpler terms, Amelia said: "I'm justice and it's too late to say you're sorry."

"Let's go!" Amelia commanded. "Yaa!"

With that, she bounded from the branch toward the ground below. *Far* below.

SPLAT!

I winced.

"Hey!" Gourry cried, wide-eyed as he knelt down to make sure Amelia wasn't knocked out. "You okay?"

Amelia spat out a twig and coughed. "No need to be concerned!" she cried as she got to her feet. Something was very wrong.

"Amelia?" I asked. "Your, uh, neck's all crooked. You okay?"

"It's all right!" Amelia declared with a dismissive wave of her hand. "It'll take more than a measly fall to break *my* spirit!"

. . . But it was plenty to break her neck?

One of the masked bandits seemed to come to his senses. "I think," he mumbled, "we shouldn't mess with these people."

Too late for that, pal, I thought. *Nobody gets out of a fight after getting Amelia worked up.*

"Prepare thyselves, servants of evil!" Amelia shouted before beginning to chant a spell.

To make a short story even shorter, the final curtain fell over that battle no sooner than it had started. Not to toot our own horns, but our blistering, offensive magic spells were more than enough to take care of a sorry gang of bandits.

"Um . . . hey," muttered Gourry after the very quick frenzy. He stood alone, dejected, idly poking his sword at the dirt behind Amelia and me. Amelia was too busy striking her Heroic Pose to notice, so I was the one to turn.

"Next time we have a chance to kick some bandit tail," Gourry asked, "could you please leave one for me?"

Quickly and firmly, I replied, "No."

Amelia and I weren't about to wait around for Gourry to get caught up with the situation. It takes the guy long enough just to tie his shoes in the morning. Besides, I wanted to grill those pitiful bandits about the whereabouts of their loot.

I grabbed the nearest crook by the collar and ripped off his ratty mask. The man under the disguise looked very unbanditlike. He wasn't ugly like your typical wart-nosed scoundrel—but let's not get carried away, he wasn't handsome, either. He was just very normal-looking.

"Hey!" I yelled as threateningly as I could. "Wake up!" I shook him by the collar a bunch of times until his eyes fluttered open.

"Uh . . . mmm?" he moaned, followed by, "yaaaagh!"

I could tell he wanted nothing more than to run in the opposite direction until his body gave out. You see what happens when you mess with Lina, kids?

"W-wait!" he stuttered. "Please! I don't wanna die!"

I cackled as diabolically as I could. "Your treasure in exchange for your life, perhaps."

They were the very words he and his sorry ilk used to filch money from innocent victims. *How do you like it, you thieving scumbag?*

"Th-that's uncalled for," the bandit whined. "How could you be so cruel?!"

That sounded particularly funny coming from a bandit.

"Where do you get off questioning *our* morals?" I railed at him. "Don't even go there! And tell me where you're stashing the stash!"

"Sorry." The voice came from somewhere behind us. "Would you mind letting that gentleman go?"

"Wha—?!" Amelia blurted as we spun around on our heels.

In the shadow of a tree, a woman stared at us calmly.

The bandit I was interrogating suddenly cried out, "M-Miss Mazenda!"

She looked around twenty years old and wore soft white clothing that accentuated her fair skin. Her long hair and lips were both glossy red and vibrantly beautiful.

She was the kind of woman lovestruck guys could call a "peerless beauty." The image of her on a snow-white mountain peak, sipping delicious sherbet, crossed my mind.

"I didn't want anyone getting hurt here."

"Er," the bandit blabbered. "Bay, over there, he put us to it and—"

"I wasn't talking to *you*," Mazenda interrupted. After cutting the man's words off with such commanding ease, she went on addressing us: "As useless as they may seem, they are in my service. Could you see it in your heart to let them go?"

She's gotta be kidding, right?

"Do you really expect us to agree to that?" I asked, raising an eyebrow.

Mazenda shook her head at my question, a wry smile on her lips. "No," she said simply, unfazed. "Hmm . . . so what shall we do about this? I'm tired of formalities. Let's settle this with fewer distractions."

As she spoke, she took a decisive step forward.

It was enough to put Amelia, Gourry, and me on our guards. Amelia leapt far to the rear while Gourry readied his hand on the hilt of his sword. As for me, I released the bandit I was interrogating and began chanting a spell.

The treetops suddenly shuddered violently. An instant later, leaves showered down on us, filling the air and almost completely obscuring our vision.

All I could squeak out was "Ugh?!"

I sensed a presence somewhere above us and looked up. Mazenda hovered high in the air, that same wry smile fixed on her lips. She held a stone in one of her hands.

Was she going to start pelting us with rocks? I wondered if she was casting some kind of warding magic. She did hurl the stone, not at me, but at the ground near me.

I immediately recoiled, leaping sideways. I soon found out that was a bad idea.

ZAP!

A weak charge of lightning struck me. For a moment, a numb, tingling sensation coursed through my limbs.

The effect didn't last long, at least. I came back to my senses fast, but I still couldn't figure out what stunt that woman was trying to pull. I rapidly chanted a spell.

"Elmekia Lance!" I shouted and released it in her direction . . .

. . . Or didn't, actually.

My head went completely blank. It was like a light had suddenly been switched off, and all those supercharged flashes of thoughts in my brain abruptly vanished.

"You appear to be the leader of this small group," Mazenda taunted, her voice drawling from somewhere behind the thick curtain of wildly dancing leaves. "So, since I've grown bored, I've decided to make you my new playmate. If you defeat me, you will be restored. Come to the village of Mane if you're interested."

Another flurry of leaves tumbled from above, the noise of their furious rustling enveloping the forest. Then, just like that, it was as quiet and peaceful as before.

Amelia, Gourry, and I stood there dumbfounded. I had no idea how, but the defeated gang of bandits had disappeared with Mazenda—it was as if we'd never run into them in the first place.

"Argh!" I snapped, gripping my temples. It felt like a walnut was knocking around inside my brain. What the hell had that woman done to me?!

"They're gone," Amelia breathed in disbelief.

"Lina?" Gourry called, sheathing his blade. "Are you all right?" As he stepped toward me, something barely snagged his foot.

"What's this?" he asked, his eyes lowering to the ground. A long, red needle poked out of the dirt path, slender and glinting in the sunlight. Gourry reached down and pulled it free; the instant he did so, the needle lost its rigidity and dangled in his fingers like string.

"It's a hair," Amelia declared in her commanding voice, which really wasn't necessary. "It's probably from that Mazenda woman."

A few quick glances were all it took to spot four more needles planted in the dirt around me. Together with the one Gourry had found, they added up to five . . . arrayed in a pentagram with me at its center.

Um, yikes.

Mazenda's big display of angry leaves had just been a feint. In the moment I'd dropped my focus, she'd created a warding field around me using her own hair as its five points.

But something else bothered me, something potentially worse. I needed to test my theory right away.

"What's wrong, Lina?" Gourry asked, probably worried about the twisted scowl on my face.

I never bothered to answer his question. I began casting a spell.

"Lighting!"

And yes, boys and girls, the absolute worst possible thing happened at that very moment.

Nothing.

"Miss Lina!" Amelia exclaimed. "What's going on?" Her face went white in the blink of an eye.

Gourry, though, still hadn't caught on. "Now Amelia's upset?" he noted like the brilliant detective he was. "What the heck's going on here?!"

With Gourry, you go half speed, if that.

The blankness inside my head confirmed the truth. I turned to Gourry, gritting my teeth so hard I practically made sparks.

"Gourry," I said very, very slowly, almost to convince myself as much as to convince him. "I . . . can't . . . cast . . . spells."

Aaaaaaaaaaaaaaaaaaaaaaaaaaaaaaaaaaaaaaaaaaaaaaaaaaaaaaaaah!

***

I didn't manage to collect my thoughts until we reached an inn near the village. I thought a good gorging would calm my nerves (the way it usually does), but my mind was so wracked with confusion and panic that not even two servings of the Special of the Day could bring me back to my senses.

"So . . . what you're telling me," Gourry said, slowly putting two and two together, "is that Lina can't use spells at all?"

"That's what it looks like." Amelia sighed.

Gourry's dim-wittedness wasn't even *vaguely* funny right then, and I was in no mood to deal with him. I let Amelia—Miss Happy to Pipe In—field his questions instead.

"Man," Gourry commented, thumping the table with his hand. "That sucks. I guess we'd better figure out a way to deal with that, huh?"

Wow, what a philosopher!

Amelia nodded vigorously. "Definitely. A Lina who can't cast spells is just . . ." She trailed off, obviously trying to find the right words.

"A pest?" Gourry offered.

My eye twitched.

Say what?

"Well, I wouldn't go that far," Amelia said. "Although she won't exactly be able to back up her attitude with any *useful* skills."

TWITCH! *Excuse me? Attitude?!*

"Her ego's huge, but her breasts are so puny," Gourry whined.

"Yeah," Amelia mumbled, chewing a carrot. "And it's not as if she's sexy in any other way to counteract—"

"SILEEEEEEENCE!" I roared. "Trying to kick me when I'm down, are ya? Keep that up and it'll cost you your teeth!"

Gourry and Amelia glanced at each other quizzically. "But . . ." Gourry began, scratching at his face.

"Please don't be angry, Miss Lina," Amelia said. "Mister Gourry and I were just saying those things to try and cheer you up."

Cheer me up? Why don't you just pour acid over me instead?!

"You little . . . !" I shrieked as I lunged.

"W-wait, Lina!" Gourry tried to jam his arms between Amelia and me. "Strangling Amelia won't solve anything! How sure are you that you can't use your spells? You really can't cast them at all?"

"Not unless I defeat Mazenda," I said, panting. "That's what *she* said, anyway." I loosened my fingers from Amelia's windpipe and quietly sat back down. Amelia cleared her throat and went back to finishing her meal.

"So it's simple, right?" Amelia raised her hand and, with a slight grimace, tried to work the kinks out of her neck. "Why don't we face off with her like she recommended? She *is* a villain, after all, because the friends of villains are villains, too. There's no need for mercy here."

Mazenda may be a villain, I wanted to tell her, *but that isn't going to make beating her any easier.* Especially considering my own situation.

"Where are we even gonna find her?" Gourry asked.

I sighed at Gourry. It took me a full half-minute to muster enough patience to answer him.

"Mane Village," I grated. "Mazenda said so herself. She said it loud enough for the unconscious *bandits* to hear, Gourry."

"Oh, I heard it loud and clear," Gourry explained. "I just forgot."

Gourry is the only guy I know who takes pride in being clueless.

Gourry shrugged. "Sounds good to me. It's on our route, right? Let's go for it."

I looked up at Gourry in shock, realizing he'd actually said something halfway intelligent. I slowly nodded. He turned to me then, his eyes suddenly serious, and I found myself actually wondering what he had to say.

Any more tidbits of insight, Gourry?

"But back to the matter at hand," he announced. He reached over and picked a not-quite-bare bone from my plate. "Do you mind if I chew on this? 'Cause there's still a lot of meat on here."

I spent the rest of the meal trying to jam that bone down his throat.

***

"Whaaaaaat?!"

Amelia's outburst shattered the calm and peaceful quiet of the inn.

"Keep it down!" the grizzled old innkeeper said in a harsh whisper, his eyes darting about the room. "You trying to alert the press or somethin'?"

The village of Mane was nestled along the old back roads that led from Saillune, through the Kingdom of Dils, and onward to Kalmaart. In other words, Mane was only two villages away from the town we stayed in that night.

I was glad we'd made it so far from Saillune, but Mane Village was Mazenda and company's stronghold. Our journey was going to get very treacherous very fast, and I sincerely doubted we could traipse into Mane and pull off an easy victory. In other words, we were going to take our sweet time making that final leg of the journey to Mane. We'd been *planning* to lodge in the village we were in—use it as a base for stocking up on information about Mane's background, making local inquiries, and "investigating" nearby hole-in-the-wall eateries—but the innkeeper hadn't started us off on the most confident note. He'd pretty much told us to avoid Mane entirely.

Hence Amelia's shrieking. She hadn't liked hearing that, y'see.

"How could you say such a thing?!" she demanded, proving for the second time in thirty seconds that she had no volume control. "If you know there is evil afoot so near your own village, how can you keep it from the local authorities? Is there no love of justice in your heart?!"

The innkeeper looked at Amelia like she'd suddenly sprouted jackass ears.

"L-love of what?" he stammered. "This isn't about justice, girlie! I told you—all that 'evil' stuff is just rumor! You think I'm gonna go to an official with rumors and no proof? I'd just get myself into a load of trouble!"

The innkeeper had a valid point, but Amelia wasn't one to be swayed by common sense.

"No, I see what's going on!" she announced. She leapt onto a wooden chair and shook her right fist high over her head. "There is a great conspiracy of evil in progress! A great vortex swirling somewhere nearby!"

If you mean a vortex of crazy swirling right above your head, then yeah.

Even Gourry was getting worried. "She's starting up again," he whined in that anguished, my-fried-chicken-got-overcooked tone.

I took Gourry by the elbow and led him to a far corner of the room. Amelia's screaming had gotten me thinking, and I wanted to talk it out—not to mention the fact that I didn't want to be seen with her during a righteousness fit.

"Listen," I muttered to Gourry under my breath. "If Amelia's reaction is anything to go by, then maybe Mane's even more dangerous than we thought. She's got a pretty good sense for evil, remember."

"Well, I dunno . . ." Gourry started, then trailed off.

"Okay," I breathed. *Remember his tiny brain,* I reminded myself. "Then why would Mazenda, as conniving as we know she is, try to bait us into that village? Are you saying we should take her words at face value?"

"Er, no," Gourry replied gingerly. "That'd be dumb."

"So what's the *problem*, Gourry?"

"Um, well . . ." Gourry couldn't come up with more than a few monosyllabic grunts as a response. Soon, he was sitting on a nearby chair, his face scrunched up in thought.

"Look at it this way," he said finally. "Everybody we've met and everything we've seen up 'til now hasn't been what we expected, right? So maybe Mane's like that—we'll think it's really bad, but then we'll go there and it'll be an ostrich ranch or something."

I could see that reasoning with Gourry was getting us nowhere. "Never mind," I groaned and dragged him back to our table.

It was around that time that Amelia returned with a very grave expression on her face.

"What is it?" I asked. But she wouldn't answer; she just shook her head.

"Not right now," she murmured. "We'll talk when we get back to our rooms."

Gourry and I looked at each other.

Okay, I thought. *Does this mean it's time to panic?*

★★★

Amelia, Gourry, and I gathered in the middle room of the three adjacent ones we'd reserved for the night. By meeting there and keeping our voices hushed, we could keep the possibility of eavesdroppers listening in on us to a minimum. The last thing we needed right then was undue attention from the locals.

"All right," I told Amelia. "Get talking."

She took a breath. "I know that this is all rumor—" she began before abruptly pausing, her jaw clenched so tight, in fact, that I thought she might break all her teeth.

"From what I've learned," she continued slowly, "a secret society is using Mane Village as its stronghold."

"We know that already." Gourry smirked. "It's the bandit group, the one that woman runs, right? Next topic!" He slapped his hands together, pleased with himself.

Let her talk, dumbass!

Amelia shook her head solemnly. "No, not them. It's a religious cult, and that woman Mazenda and her bandits are probably just followers."

"A religious cult?" I repeated, my eyebrows raised.

"Yes. But listen to this." She swallowed. "The man downstairs called it the Cult of Shabranigdu."

"C-Cult of Shabranigdu?!" I shrieked.

Ruby Eye Shabranigdu, the Demon Lord believed to be the master of all darkness in the world. The insanely evil bastard we'd had a hell of a time fighting in the past.

"Shh! Your voice is too loud!" Amelia berated.

"Sorry." I furrowed my eyebrows. "Amelia, are you *sure* this info's good?"

"Who knows?" Amelia replied with a resigned shrug. "As the innkeeper said earlier, it's all rumor. But it sounds pretty suspicious to me. I mean, why would people in an obviously fear-riddled town just make up a Cult of Shabranigdu? That's probably the most frightening and evil thing I can think of."

I pondered that for a minute, but I wasn't connecting the dots between this rumored cult and Mazenda baiting me into Mane.

"What's your point?" I came out and asked.

Amelia thought about that for a moment, then said, "That's it," with a light-hearted smile.

Yes, she actually smiled. I resisted the urge to wipe it off her face.

"All the innkeeper knows," Amelia continued, "is that Mane is supposedly the center for the cult and that there's a good chance evil's going on. But that's all he's heard; I think that's all he *wants* to hear."

I frowned. The scenario was getting more and more complicated, and not in that good, tangled-up-with-an-excess-of-unclaimed-jewels way.

"Lina?" Gourry piped in. He'd been completely silent up until then, no doubt daydreaming about his next battle or meal. "Something she said before is beginning to bug me."

"What is it?" I asked, bracing myself for a mind-bendingly stupid question.

"Shabunigrado. Just what is that?"

And he didn't let me down. You can always count on Gourry for some things.

"Shabranigdu, Mister Gourry?" Amelia corrected him. Even she seemed stunned by Gourry's brain mush, since she turned to me with an "is he all right?" look.

Gourry was oblivious to it, though, and sat there scratching his head.

"Mmm," he mumbled. "I feel like I've heard that name before. I'm really bad with names, especially long ones like that."

27

"Gourry, you moronic—!" I managed to hold the rest of my words back.

"Whoa," Gourry protested. "Lina, it's not like it's a big deal or anything. It's just a name, right?"

"Of course it's a big deal!" I shouted. "How can you not remember Shabranigdu?!"

"Er . . ." Gourry trailed off. "Well, uh . . ."

"The Demon Lord!" I snarled. "The personification of evil! Red eyes, yea tall, churning with the malice of a thousand dying worlds?!"

After mulling over this information for a moment, Gourry nodded and smacked his palm with his fist. "Oh, yeah," he declared. "That dude. I remember now."

Gourry's not just a dimwit, he's also a liar.

"I wonder what this cult's all about?" I ventured. "What are they after? I doubt they're out to organize a symposium on evil with the Demon Lord as their guest of honor."

"I did catch wind of one thing," Amelia whispered ominously. "Apparently, their evil beliefs require them to make material sacrifices to satisfy the Demon Lord's greed."

Hmm. If that were true, the bandits were suddenly beginning to make sense. First, you overrun a perfectly peaceful and prosperous village. Then, to serve the Demon Lord's lust for possession, you plunder the townsfolk for all they're worth before rampaging through the countryside and looting from everyone you can.

"If this cult does exist," I said, "then the bandits we tangled with earlier are all members of it, right?"

"That's exactly what I think!" Amelia said excitedly. She thrust her fist triumphantly into the air. "No matter how many people have lost their way and given themselves over to the darkness, no matter how many people have joined this cult and sacrificed common decency for a sense of belonging, we need not fear!" She stood now, assuming that heroic pose again. "So long as justice exists, victory shall undoubtedly embrace us!"

Gourry spat a fingernail out of his mouth. "But that's gonna be tough without Lina using magic."

"Right," I said. "About that." I promptly began chanting a spell.

"Lighting!"

At the end of my fingertip, I did notice a faint shimmer of light. But it vanished almost immediately, leaving us all to stare at a dainty but otherwise uninteresting finger.

"Hey!" Amelia twittered. "I saw something!"

I nodded at her. "I admit that was pretty pathetic for a lighting spell, but it did prove that the pentagram's ward seems to be weakening." I sighed. "Unfortunately," I went on, "Lighting is all I can manage right now. I can forget about attack spells; I'll barely be able to work up a puff of wind."

"Cheer up," Gourry said happily as he patted me on the back. "Doesn't that mean your powers are gonna return to normal eventually? Just give it some time."

"It's not that simple," I moped. "A complete recovery could take years! And even then, there's no guarantee I'll get all my spells back." I clenched my fists. Stupid Mazenda!

"Anyway, we need to do our homework first. Someone has to check up on any rumors regarding the cult's hideout and gather whatever info's available on Mane. That's quite a job, isn't it, Gourry?"

Gourry looked up from staring at the floor. "What do you mean by that?"

"Oh, you know," I said as casually as I could. "First of all, I'm absolutely certain our enemy's been informed of what we look like. So, whatever we do, we'll have to do it under the cover of darkness."

Gourry frowned. "And?"

"And darkness is beauty's greatest foe," I said, hoping to stump Gourry by sounding profound.

Beside me, Amelia nodded at my words. She knew what I was getting at, but Gourry had checked out again.

"Uh . . ." Gourry's eyebrows knotted up so tightly he could have easily passed for the village idiot.

Sensing that I'd confused Gourry past the point of no return, I struck while the iron was hot: "So, I must humbly appoint he who is least burdened by fairness of face and body to fulfill the task at hand. That makes you our brave investigator, Gourry. Congrats!"

Gourry blinked. "H-hold on," he mumbled feebly. "What do you take me for, a ranger? You think I tramp around mountain ranges every night snooping around for stuff?"

"Ho ho!" I laughed with a wink at Gourry. "You're certainly built for it!"

"Don't you dare! Even *I* know how dangerous that kind of scouting is. You can't trick me with all that fancy talking and think I'll go just 'cause *you* said so . . ." Gourry's words petered out. He sat there, panting, while I scratched my head and tried to devise a new strategy.

"You've got a point, Gourry," I finally admitted. "This isn't my decision to make. If we decide on it properly, as a group, then will you still have a problem?"

"Well, no," Gourry said sheepishly. "I'd be fine with it if we decided all fair-like."

And just like that, I spring my trap!

"Okay," I said, "we'll vote! Everyone who thinks Gourry should be our investigator, raise your hand."

Amelia and I both shot our hands up.

"Then it's settled." I smiled at Gourry. "Good luck!"

"Hey!"

"Mister Gourry," Amelia murmured. She frowned solemnly and patted him on the shoulder. "I do feel the anguish in your heart, but know that you are serving the higher forces of democracy." She even sniffled.

Never one to betray his manliness, Gourry straightened up and choked back tears. I was starting to feel bad for the guy when he suddenly brightened.

"Ha!" he cried triumphantly, pointing a finger in my face. "You've gone soft, Lina! Your scheme has one fatal flaw!"

"W-what?!" My schemes never have flaws, so I had to take offense.

He stood up proudly and crossed his arms. "Do you really think sending me, who has no idea what's going on, is going to get us anywhere?" he scoffed. "What do you take me for?"

It was like a hammer had been thrown full-force at my head. "Yikes!" I hollered, nearly falling out of my chair. Gourry, being astute? "You're scaring me, Gourry. Could this mean that your brains are finally taking shape?"

"Now, wait just a . . ." Gourry scowled and wagged a finger at me. "Don't talk about people's brains like they're breasts!"

Okay, we can see where this guy's been putting his brainpower.

I'd just thought up a witty comeback to Gourry's breast obsession when the door to our room flew open. The nearly dehinged wood surface slammed against the wall, sending all of us reaching for our weapons.

"Excuse me!" snarled our uninvited guest. "Could you please be a little quieter in here?"

The innkeeper, burly and snorting, stood in our doorway with his arms folded. It was quite an intimidating sight, let me tell you. All the three of us could think to do was apologize— very quietly.

In the end, we decided who would play investigator using the only tried-and-true method known to intelligent life: rock-paper-scissors. Too bad we all chose rock.

Countless torches flickered in the darkness. Their tiny flames illuminated a large arena, its bowed walls looming over an assembly of hundreds of masked men.

"There's a lot more here than I counted on," I whispered.

We'd made our way deep inside a mountain range not far from Mane. The coliseum we were hiding in had probably been impressive in its earlier days, but the slow erosion of time—not to mention human neglect—had left it a chipped, decrepit ruin.

A sloping array of tiered benches circled the large internal region, and more than half the seats had already crumbled away; those that remained intact were all occupied by the masked men.

The three of us perched on the uppermost part of the coliseum's sides, furthest from the proceedings taking place below. Those higher tiers had suffered the most wear and were pretty much unreachable—unless, of course, you knew how to use levitation. Not only did that mean no sentries, but the shadows and our sheer height made us practically invisible to anyone below. Amelia had spotted the ruins the night before. I silently reminded myself to give her a cookie later.

"Those guys don't look like much to me," Gourry muttered.

"I thought the cult would only have a few members," I explained, "but this is incredible. Their beliefs must be pretty popular if they can get a crowd all the way out here."

"Incredible is right," Amelia snapped. "Adherents of evil in a place as venerated as this? Does the word *justice* have no meaning here?!" Her hands curled into fists. "I cannot forgive this!"

I ignored her. You learn to do that after a while.

We waited and watched the assembly below us. A few minutes later, the masked crowd erupted into cheers.

"Someone's coming out!" Gourry exclaimed, stating the obvious.

And that, folks, is why we love him!

Five men appeared from a corridor once used by coliseum combatants. Their robes and mantles were deep red, and they each brandished executioner's swords with blades steeped in the same crimson. While the first four of them wore masks—all of them red, of course—the face of the fifth and last man was uncovered. The masks that they wore were different from those worn by the crowd members; the style of mask probably denoted rank.

The bare-faced man walked to the center of the arena. The other four positioned themselves about six paces away from him, each faced outward in the four points of the compass: north, south, east, and west.

"I see," Amelia snarled disgustedly. "The five retainers!"

"Retainers?" Gourry mumbled. "The heck's that?" He looked in my direction, so I obliged him with a basic explanation.

"They're five high-ranking Mazoku, the ones Ruby Eye Shabranigdu gave birth to." I didn't know if the story was truth or legend, but I knew it by heart just the same. What can I say? I'm a sucker for a good yarn.

"Yeah," Amelia joined in. "The outer four represent Chaos Dragon, Deep Sea, Dynast, and Greater Beast." She took a deep breath, then added, "And the man at the center is Hellmaster. The names are based on their positions."

I wondered, though, if the man at the center could really be the cult's founder. He was thin by anybody's standards. He looked, in fact, like some half-starved, third-rate sorcerer villain, right down to his complete lack of charisma.

"Gentlemen!" the man boomed. Contrary to his weakling appearance, his voice was surprisingly buff. "I have good news for you today! Master Krotz will return to us very soon!"

An upsurge of cheers filled the entire coliseum. From the ecstatic response, I could only guess that this Krotz fellow was the group's leader. So what did that make the skinny chump addressing the assembly? A fill-in?

"Moreover," the speaker continued, "I have been advised that he has obtained that which we seek!" His voice took on a zealous, if somewhat uptight, tone. The cheers that followed were even louder and more ecstatic.

"Now none can oppose us! The hypocrites worshipping Ceiphied and the other false gods shall know their error! With true power, all that we desire shall be ours!"

This guy sure likes the sound of his own voice.

I stole a quick glance at Amelia to see how she was holding up. The girl was prone to blowing her top at the slightest provocation, and the last thing we needed right then was an Amelia-sized debacle. I saw her mumbling to herself, her face sullen, but she was keeping a lid on it.

The man below continued his speech: "The nature of existence is contradictory, and therefore evil. We cannot tolerate such a—"

And that's when Amelia released the lid. She suddenly bolted straight up and began wreaking havoc.

"Burst Rond!"

Dozens of balls of blazing light sprang up around her, then plunged down into the arena.

KA-BOOOOOM!

"Yaaaaah!" a masked follower screamed.

"Yiiiii!" another cried out, tumbling off his tier and into the benches below.

Flames and shrieks erupted from one end of the meeting place to the other. It was pandemonium!

I immediately sank down where I was crouched and covered my head. *Dammit!* I thought. *I should've known better!*

Amelia's earlier mumbling hadn't been her trying to contain her rage but, rather, her chanting a no-holds-barred attack spell. Here's a piece of advice: if you're going to let loose with attack spells, at least give your companions some kind of *warning* before you unleash.

Now, before you get the impression that the fusillade of fireballs created by that spell blew the place to smithereens, listen up. The power was on the low end of the scale, so the damage was very localized—direct hits made blackened toast, but indirect ones didn't do much. Unfortunately, it was quite enough to make a statement, and that statement was simple: Amelia, on behalf of the three of us, had declared war on the Cult of Shabranigdu.

***

It wasn't long before we were spotted.

"Look up there!" I heard one of the cult members cry out.

"I can see someone!" another hollered. "Have we no lookouts?"

At that instant, Amelia sprang into action again. I wasn't sure I wanted her to spring into action again.

"Lighting!" she shouted. The spell illuminated a large chunk of sky directly above her.

"Listen well, all ye who worship the darkness!" she shouted at the scrambling people below. "No matter how many deceptions besiege us, there is but one truth! If there is even one of you with the light of truth in his heart, realize the wickedness of the path you have chosen and choose the right course—of your own free will!"

"Dispose of them!" the speaker demanded.

Big surprise there.

As soon as the beanpole gave the word, the "believers" thronged and proceeded toward us. But they could only go so far; as I said, the place we'd chosen for our stakeout was pretty much unreachable, so all the believers could do was rail, stamp their feet, and watch us helplessly.

"Amelia!" I shouted. "Gourry! We need to make a tactical retreat!"

"Why?!" Amelia protested. "We can fight them all here and—"

"We can't fight on this footing!" I shot back, cutting Amelia off mid-sentence. "What do we do if one of them can use attack spells? The tier below us is unsteady as it is!"

"B-but showing our backs to the enemy . . ." Amelia complained.

"Bear momentary disgrace, fall back, return again and counterattack!" I told her emphatically, recalling words that were hammered into me when I'd been a sorceress-in-training. *Guess I did pay attention to one or two things back in school.*

"That's what Champions of Justice do!" I added encouragingly.

The fury left Amelia's eyes. "You're right!" she declared, her tone swiftly changing from angry to inspired. "That's absolutely true!" And with that, she immediately began chanting another spell.

I was lucky Amelia's goodness also made her extremely easy to manipulate.

"Levitation!" she cried. Amelia's spell lifted the three of us into the sky.

"Sorcery?!" a man below yelled, half angry and half shocked.

"Why, you!" another roared. "You won't get away! Everybody head out!" The countless masked men fell all over each other as they rushed for the nearest exits.

They were beginning to make me nervous. "Hurry, Amelia!"

"This is as fast as we can go!" she argued as we floated out of there and above the trees.

Gourry didn't say a word, but he didn't have to. The sweat dripping off his forehead said it all.

As a spell, Levitation has excellent maneuverability, but in using it you're sacrificing speed; it only goes about as fast as a walking adult. As we floated toward the ground, I saw that our pursuers were already advancing on us.

"Into the forest!" Amelia yelled. She took off running as she spoke, not even bothering to make sure Gourry and I followed. From behind us, we heard the run-of-the-mill lines that all pursuers use: "Let's go!" and "Over here!" Under the circumstances, I wasn't about to dock points from our pursuers for not using original lines;

the giant mob was threatening enough, and that lit the fire under our butts to keep us racing through the woods.

Suddenly, Amelia veered off the path and into the trees.

"Both of you, hands!" she called out, reaching toward us with one of her own. Gourry and I gripped it. Amelia, it seemed, had already chanted her spell and was ready to go, but as spells go, it was a rather unusual one, and it certainly brought to mind not the most pleasant memory.

"Dark Mist!" The moment she said it, the world went pitch black.

You can't see your hand in front of your face in a Dark Mist. Of course, that also meant that none of our pursuers could see us. We fumbled in the blackness, but at least we were safely hidden.

A certain assassin used that spell on me once. I realized its potential, but it also made me queasy.

"Amelia!" I called to her. "When did you learn that?"

I could sense her smile in the darkness. "It seemed like a useful spell, so I practiced it in secret."

"Nice!" I said with a chuckle. "Your father would blow a gasket if he found out. Gourry, you should be more proactive like Amelia."

I heard Gourry grunt, "But—" or something along those lines.

"There!" a voice from outside the Dark Mist field shouted. "I hear voices!"

Gourry cut whatever he was saying short as we realized just how close our pursuers were. All three of us clammed up in a big hurry.

"Over here!" another cried. "I definitely heard voices this waaaa—?!"

"What's wro—whoa! What's this black stuff doing here in the middle of the woods?!"

It sounded like Dark Mist had thrown our pursuers off our trail. In the glow of torches, the mist had probably appeared as nothing more than a great amorphous blackness. I was sure they were weirded out.

Way to go, Amelia!

"I'm inside it!" a panicky voice cried. "I can't see a damn thing in here! It has to be some sort of sorcery!"

"Yeek!" another yelled. "Somebody call Lady Mazenda!"

"She's at the temple!" a different pursuer shot back.

The temple, eh? Now we're getting somewhere.

***

"Hey, Lina!" Gourry called. "You plan to stop running anytime soon?"

We were by then more than two villages past Mane. None of us had said anything before Gourry's sudden question; we'd been so busy hotfooting it from that gang of masked creeps that we hadn't bothered to think of what to do next. We'd been on our feet without a single break for hours.

"That's right," Amelia squealed, panting. "It'll be dawn soon. Can we take a break, please?" She did look ready to collapse any second.

"Fine," I replied. "We'll rest at the next village, okay?"

I was pretty wiped out myself, and my feet were sore as hell. Gourry amazed me, though; even after all the running, he seemed totally composed and didn't show any signs of slowing down. The man was a machine.

All I cared about was putting as much distance between the enemy and us as was humanly possible. Of course, there was always the option of camping in the forest, but Amelia and I vetoed that idea damn fast. No camping for us.

"While we're talking," Amelia chirped exhaustedly (if that's even possible), "what have you been thinking about since we left that place, Miss Lina? A counterattack plan, I hope."

"Wouldn't we have been better off fighting those guys back there?" Gourry asked. "We could've destroyed them all in one shot."

Gourry thought like a toddler, and I was used to that, but seeing Amelia nod so energetically at his suggestion was disappointing. Sleep deprivation must've been fogging up her head.

"First of all," I reasoned with them, "smashing that meeting place to smithereens would've accomplished nothing. Don't you remember? Their leader was away somewhere; the guy making the speech said so."

"You mean that wasn't their headquarters?" Gourry asked, his face all screwed up with puzzlement.

"Ugh," I groaned. "Gourry, since when does a broken-down monstrosity like that coliseum make a good home base? Even if it *is* hidden in the forest, it'd get found as soon as someone ventured even a little ways into the mountains. Besides, don't you remember one of those masked guys saying that Mazenda was at a temple?"

"A temple? Someone said that?"

I suddenly felt like banging my head against the nearest tree.

"Yes!" I fumed. "Mazenda wasn't anywhere to be seen when Amelia set off her fireworks. So, logically, this place they call 'the temple' is somewhere other than where the cult met. Are you following me?" I squinted my eyes and braced for his answer.

Gourry thought about this. "So the temple's their headquarters, then."

"Good." I sighed with relief. "At any rate, defeating Mazenda and restoring my magic powers have to top our priority list right now. You follow me, right?"

Gourry raised his finger and cocked his chin skyward. "Ahhhh," he said, then quite simply added, "No."

"Gourry!"

"Wait," he interjected, his tone becoming more urgent. "Look at Amelia."

"Amelia?" I repeated, then turned.

What the hell?

Amelia just stood there, motionless, her arms slack at her sides as she stared into space. Gourry strode over to her and passed his hand back and forth in front of her face. He snapped his fingers inches from her nose.

"Don't worry," he said at last. "She just went to sleep standing up. We should leave her be for a bit."

"Excuse me?" I stomped over to Gourry. "We're in no place to 'leave her be,' genius. Use that glop between your ears every once in a while."

I turned to Amelia. "Hey!" I shouted. "Amelia! I'm talking to you!" I shook her by the shoulders several times until her eyelids fluttered open.

"Ah," she warbled like a little bird. "Miss Lina."

"Not used to all-nighters?"

"No," she bubbled. "I'm a . . . sound . . . sleeper."

You don't say.

"Then we don't have a choice," I decided. "Gourry, you're gonna have to carry her on your back."

But by then Gourry was laid out and snoring.

"ARGH!" I cried. "Get up, you idiot! This isn't the place for a nap!"

My yelling snapped him awake. "You're right," Gourry agreed, yawning and getting to his feet. "It isn't." In that split second, though, the expression on his face suddenly got very intense. He'd drawn his blade without my even realizing it.

In the next moment, I knew why—I sensed a presence. It had taken me awhile to catch on to it; I was more tired than I'd realized.

"An enemy?" Amelia asked. Her eyes, too, had gone alert and shone with focus. The sense of danger had completely startled the sleep out of her.

The boughs of the trees before us rustled.

"Lina, listen to me," Gourry said under his breath. "Take Amelia and get out of here. I'll stay and hold them off."

"A-are you nuts?" I stammered in disbelief. "Are you even sure we're under attack?!"

"Yeah, and I can tell they're not amateurs. You can't cast spells, and Amelia doesn't have an ounce of strength left. Let me take care of 'em."

"Ah," someone cawed from the trees. "A rather optimistic outlook, wouldn't you say?"

The voice was high-pitched and male. We peered into the shadows of the forest, but I couldn't see anyone. Whoever was about to ambush us was well hidden.

"Stop hiding like a cowardly villain and show yourself!" Amelia yelled, but the presence in the woods didn't even bother to respond to her.

A long, tense silence passed before the male voice spoke again. "I admire your gall in picking a fight back at the assembly while we were not present," it commented. "You were lucky to have evaded us then, but your luck has now come to an end. All you managed to do was delay your own death." The voice suddenly began to cackle.

I'm sorry, did I miss something funny?

"Gilfa," growled a second voice. "You talk too much."

Unlike the first voice, I could actually see who—or, rather, *what*—spoke: a beast-man. At first glance, he resembled a lizard man, but a closer look revealed some telling differences. If the large bulge on his back was anything to go by, he was probably some hybrid of a black cobra and a human.

Slung low in one of his hands was a great sword. Its blade was tall enough to reach the top of Gourry's head; very impressive-looking, I had to admit.

"How unsociable of you, Vedur," chortled the one whose name was Gilfa. "I simply want the short-lived humans to know what they're dealing with."

"Irrelevant," snarled Vedur, the beast-man. "Our orders were 'pursue and kill.' Fulfilling that is our job. Being sociable wastes time."

Vedur began to stride menacingly out from the cover of the trees. That's when I noticed Gourry carefully sheathing his sword back into his scabbard and pulling a needle out of a side pocket. That was going to come as a big surprise to our guests: the Sword of Light!

***

A little background? But of course. A long time ago, when Sairaag was known as the City of Sorcery, the Demon Beast Zanaffar razed the place. It's said that Zanaffar was destroyed by a legendary sword, one able to channel the will and energy of its bearer through its blade and thus cleave the Demon Beast in half. And yes, for the slower members of the audience—I'm talking about the Sword of Light.

Although he tended to strike people as a dunderhead, Gourry did happen to be the rightful inheritor of the Sword of Light—an extremely *skilled* inheritor, in fact.

To call on a weapon like that automatically meant Gourry deemed the situation pretty dangerous. Our assailants hadn't yet impressed me very much, but I guessed Gourry saw something in them that I didn't.

"Lina!" Gourry warned. "Amelia! Don't get careless!" He didn't take his eyes off Vedur. "There's a third guy out there!"

I blinked. A third?

"My, my," Gilfa cooed. "Impressive. Did you hear that, Vedur? Grouj is completely hidden, and yet this fellow here can still detect his presence." Gilfa's tone was so lighthearted you'd think he was hosting an afternoon tea party. "Very impressive, indeed."

Guessing from the direction of Gilfa's voice, he was situated right next to Vedur—but Vedur was clearly standing alone. Unless one of our assailants was a professional ventriloquist, I couldn't see how Gilfa could throw his voice so perfectly. My gaze darted around for signs of the unseen enemy.

Slowly, power began to surge through Vedur's body, and that's when all the commotion started.

"Flare Arrow!" Amelia shouted.

I'd been so busy looking for the invisible Gilfa that I hadn't noticed her chanting a spell.

KA-BOOM!

I was impressed. A couple of minutes earlier Amelia had fallen asleep standing up, yet now she fired several direct-hit shots to Vedur's body. The instant the shots hit, Gourry sprinted straight for Vedur!

"Light come forth!" Gourry boomed. Drawing forth the Sword of Light, he sliced both Vedur and his great sword right in two.

At least, that's how it *should've* gone.

"Huh?" Gourry grunted, a mixture of pain and confusion in his voice. He gasped and stumbled back, trying to catch his breath. That's when I noticed the heavy gash in his iron serpent scale breastplate.

What the hell?! I thought. I was groggy, maybe, but I knew what I saw.

The moment Gourry had drawn the Sword of Light, Vedur's shadow had erupted out of the ground and attacked Gourry with several shadow blades. While Gourry had cut through the blades with his Sword of Light, Vedur had swung his great sword and gashed Gourry's breastplate.

"Ha ha!" Gilfa cackled. "Look at that, Vedur! The Sword of Light! I'm not sure about his skill, but that blade puts your own sword to shame!" Gilfa giggled some more. "It even cleaved right through my shadow!"

Something was obviously hilarious to that guy. I was glad *someone* was having fun.

"Not a bad effort," Gilfa prattled on with malicious delight, "but you've miscalculated, I'm afraid. A spell like that won't make a dent in Vedur's body."

Just what we needed. Vedur, it seemed, had the magic resistance of a lesser demon. I'd confronted a beast-man with the same type of magic resistance before, but it was still bad news.

"Silence!" the beast-man roared at Gilfa.

My thoughts exactly.

"Oh!" Gilfa hooted. "Don't be that way, Vedur. If I hadn't used my shadow, your sword would be in pieces. And where would you be without your sword? Dead, I should think."

I was starting to guess that Gilfa was a Shadow Master. *This day just keeps getting better and better.*

"Either way," Gilfa continued, "our opponents don't stand a chance." And then he went on giggling.

"It takes one to know one!" Gourry grunted defiantly as he leapt to his feet. With that thoroughly nonsensical reply, he rushed again for Vedur.

I was still confused with Gilfa. No matter how expertly skilled a Shadow Master is, I'd never known one with the ability to speak through another's shadow. Was it possible?

"Mister Gourry!" Amelia shouted. "The shadow!"

"I'm on it!" Gourry cried back as he broke into a sprint, the Sword of Light hefted high over his head. Before I knew it, he was already upon Vedur's shadow and plunging his sword into . . . well, into the spot of ground where Vedur's shadow lay.

Vedur took the opportunity and slashed his great sword down in an overhead strike. Gourry parried it with unbelievable speed and, even better than that, managed to hew Vedur's sword in half like he was slicing through warm butter.

That's when Vedur's left fist smashed squarely into Gourry's belly.

"Agggh!" Gourry gasped.

"Gourry!" I cried.

Vedur's punch sent Gourry flying backward quite a ways. As Gourry skidded across the ground, Vedur made a beeline straight for him, but Gourry was too fast—by the time Vedur got to him, Gourry had recovered his senses enough to jump up and regrip his Sword of Light.

Vedur backed away. Without his own sword, he probably knew he didn't stand a chance against Gourry.

"Rather bumbling of you, Vedur," Gilfa said with a note of annoyance in his voice. "Now we've got no choice but to call on Grouj's power."

"No choice," the beast-man agreed in a pained tone.

"You mean the shadow wasn't him?" Amelia blurted out. She'd clearly thought that Grouj resided in Vedur's shadow.

"Run!" Gourry shouted at us. "Both of you, just go! I'll take care of these guys myself!" I noticed blood trickling from the corner of his mouth.

"No way!" I shot back. "You're bleeding!"

"I just bit my tongue! Now get outta here!"

It went against every fiber of my being, but I knew what I had to do. "All . . . right," I grunted.

"Miss Lina?"

As much as I hated to admit it, Gourry was right. "There's no point in us staying," I told Amelia. "Your spells won't do a damn thing here, and as for me, I'm . . . I'm a liability right now. I'll only get in the way."

Saying that last part was like twisting a knife in my gut, but there it was. Despite my other fighting skills, with my primary power—my magic—sealed up, I knew I'd be of no use to Gourry.

Amelia frowned worriedly but didn't argue.

"Gourry!" I shouted "We're gone!"

"I'll catch up with you later!" he yelled back. "Amelia, take care of Lina!" Gourry glanced back at me with a hint of worry in his eyes. He did his best to smile bravely, then whipped back around and brandished his sword at Vedur.

"Let's get this over with, ugly. Bring out your number three guy and we'll fight this fair and square!"

"Very well," Vedur snarled. "Grouj! Come!"

As Vedur shouted his order, a shape leapt out from the forest. It was the last thing I saw as Amelia and I retreated as fast as our weary legs could carry us.

***

"Miss Lina?" Amelia's normally upbeat tone sounded way more worried and earnest than usual.

She and I panted in a thick grove of trees. It was a secluded little place, one that seemed safe enough for cooling our heels. We'd veered into the woods just off the dirt road.

I still felt awful. How could I have left Gourry alone by himself? *It was the only way*, I kept telling myself, but that didn't calm the knots in my stomach.

"Miss Lina?" Amelia asked again.

"Oh, sorry," I mumbled. "I'm trying to figure out the best course of action for us. Give me a sec, okay?"

I went over the facts again and again, but there was no getting around it: I had to defeat Mazenda to regain my spells, but I didn't have a chance in hell without *using* those spells. And if Amelia went up against Mazenda, she'd probably just suffer the same fate I had.

That left Gourry. Only he stood a chance in a battle against Mazenda, but right then, I didn't want to think about Gourry. It only got me worrying again.

"All right," I said at last, trying not to lose my grip. "Let's hide out for a while, then we'll look for Gourry. Rendezvousing with him is our top priority."

"How unfortunate that you'll be dead long before that," said a man's voice.

We'd heard that voice before. It came from directly ahead.

"Dammit!" I muttered, gritting my teeth as I noticed the red robe and matching mantle. His gaunt face and pale eyes didn't do much to intimidate, but I wasn't taking any chances. Looks can be deceiving.

By the way, it was the thin guy from that night—the one who'd given an ecstatic speech to his assembly of jerks.

"Though I, Balgumon, may not look it," the man intoned, "I am the organization's second-in-command. While I preside over the association, I cannot tolerate such an assault as occurred this past night, and I am thus left with only one choice: to defeat you and restore my good name, a duty that must be fulfilled in the appropriate place."

Man, is this guy a windbag.

He claimed to be the cult's number two. One thing was for sure: his organization wasn't very organized, considering how easy it was to throw it into complete turmoil.

"I'm sorry," I replied flatly, "but we're gonna have to turn down your request." I sneakily drew my short sword from my hip.

You don't want to tangle with Lina Inverse in a fight, with or without my magic powers. With nothing but a sword I could take on a good four or five ne'er-do-wells in any alley in any city on any day of the week.

Did that mean I stood a chance against Slim Jim? Probably not—unless he was just an average sorcerer, in which case . . . maybe.

"Amelia!" I called over my shoulder. "Cover me!"

And with that, I charged Balgumon with my naked sword ready. I could hear Amelia cast a spell behind me.

"Bah," Balgumon snarled. "Come, then." He began chanting his own spell.

Too bad for him, Amelia was already done. She let her spell fly.

"Take this!" I hollered with my blade held high. The second before my intended slice, I dove abruptly to the side and squeezed my eyes shut.

I could feel Amelia's maximum-brightness, zero-duration lighting spell envelope the clearing in brilliant light. I was glad I'd guessed her strategy—and even more glad to hear Balgumon curse and slap his hands over his face.

Now's my chance! The instant the light waned, I whipped around and dashed straight for Balgumon. I slashed at him with a shout, timing my attack as precisely as I could.

Imagine how bummed I was when my blade only caught air.

"What?!" I cried.

Balgumon should've been completely blinded by the lighting spell, but he still dodged my attack with embarrassing ease. I recovered my balance and quickly chased after him.

Had he faked the first blindness? I could tell he was chanting a spell even as I tore through the undergrowth after him. The guy was a shifty one, so I wasn't about to cut him any slack. Charging directly at him and giving him the least amount of time for an evasive maneuver was still the best plan I could come up with.

"Miss Lina!" Amelia yelled, a jolt of unusual panic in her voice.

As soon as she spoke, I sensed another attacker streaking overhead—and boy, was he mad. I grunted and leapt to one side as rapidly as I could, watching as a silver light flared downward and cracked open the earth I'd been standing on a moment before. If my evasion had been a fraction of a second later, my head would've been split open like an unsuspecting watermelon.

"Another one?" I yelped. I got to my feet and tried to put some distance between Balgumon and me.

"Hmph!" the new attacker huffed. "She dodged it!"

He was another beast-man, only hairier than Vedur and armed with a long sword. At first glance he looked like an ordinary werewolf, but I suspected a closer inspection—which I had no intention of making—would reveal physical subtleties that would prove me wrong. Like Vedur, he was probably a hybrid.

"That wasn't necessary, Feltis," Balgumon snapped. Feltis' appearance had interrupted his spell chant.

"Are your eyes okay, then?" Feltis asked.

"Yes," Balgumon answered impatiently. "I can see well enough to take care of these fools."

As he spoke, the beast-man closed in, planting his nasty self between Balgumon and me. I brought up my sword in preparation for whatever attack he had in mind.

"Oi!" I cried. "Amelia! Take your kiddie gloves off! Show no mercy, you hear me?!"

"Understood!" Amelia cried back. With that, she began chanting another spell.

The way I saw it, we had only one shot at winning that fight, and it would take everything that Amelia had. Unfortunately, Balgumon was smart enough to not just stand around and wait to get hit. Before Amelia could finish chanting, he started running straight for her!

"Amelia!" I cried. The beast-man blocked my path so I couldn't intercept Balgumon; Amelia was on her own. Seeing Balgumon charging toward her, she quickly adopted a fighting stance.

"Don't worry, Miss Lina!" she shouted. "One villain or two, it doesn't matter; in the end, they shall all know the power of just—oof!"

Balgumon slammed a knee into Amelia's solar plexus. She promptly buckled, her face twisted in pain, and dropped to the ground like a sack of bricks.

"Don't move!" Balgumon ordered as he grappled with Amelia from behind.

I began to sweat. *Easy, Lina,* I told myself. *Just think for a second. Think!*

I wondered if I could bluff our way out of the suddenly delicate situation. I decided to try it.

"Yeah, right," I snapped. "What difference would it make if I cooperated with you? My partner and I would both get killed in the end. If anything, I oughta let loose with my sword right now, no holds barred!"

Balgumon smirked at my words. "Now, wait just a moment," he drawled carefully. "Maybe I can offer you a better option. Let me first ask, are you the sorceress whose magic Mazenda sealed?"

There was no way around it. "I am," I conceded, lowering my sword. There was no point hiding that rather glaring fact. Somebody as familiar with magic as Balgumon had probably been able to figure it out easily.

"Then another question," Balgumon continued. "This girl referred to you as 'Lina' before. Would you be *that* Lina Inverse?"

"Yes," I groaned. "I'm probably *that* Lina Inverse." This may not be the best time to mention it, but I was becoming something of a celebrity sorceress. Word of my name and deeds—as notorious as they both were—had reached far and wide. Pardon the lack of modesty here, but I'd developed quite a reputation for my wild and crazy adventures, both magic and non–magic related.

"Hmm," Balgumon murmured. "In that case, I shall spare your life, and I shall tell Mazenda to remove the seal."

I blinked. *Say what?!*

"But in return . . ." he continued.

Oh, here we go. There's always a catch when the bad guys offer favors.

". . . you shall become one of us."

All right, *hell* no. I knew I'd rather die than join a cult that worshipped Ruby Eye; not only was the troop evil, but every member I'd come in contact with had been insufferably annoying. But I didn't particularly want them to kill Amelia and me, either—that meant we'd both die petty, trivial deaths inflicted by petty, trivial enemies. And I think I deserve to die far more gloriously than that, don't you?

They had me backed into a corner. I sighed with deep resignation, but before I could agree to their terms, a voice called out from the trees.

"Ah! Mister Feltis! I've finally found you at long last!"

The voice was carefree and even personable. It was the friendliest voice I'd heard in a long time.

"Y-you!" Feltis raged. "You filthy priest! You came after me all the way *here?!*"

Obviously, Feltis wasn't feeling the love; he and the filthy priest, whatever his name was, had some bad blood between them. All the better for me! I turned to get a look at the guy I hoped would be my ally by default.

2: HUMAN LIFE: MEET, DEPART, RINSE, REPEAT

There, in a small clearing, stood a young man. He looked around twenty years old and seemed of medium stature—neither too short nor tall, thin nor fat—with a head of silky black hair cropped just below his chin. He wore the black robes common to all priests and held a priest's staff that looked right out of the discount bin. I considered his features fairly handsome, though there wasn't anything remarkable about them save for the rather out-of-place smile on his lips.

"Who is this?" sneered Balgumon. If Balgumon didn't know who the guy was, then our mystery man wasn't an ally of the Mazoku cult. Then who . . .

"We have a history," Feltis snapped, "which I'm going to close the book on by chopping him into little pieces." With that, Feltis began slowly striding forward. His eyes flared with bloodlust, and I was surprised to not see steam spurting out of his ears.

I was as baffled as Balgumon and Amelia—but, speaking for myself, I had absolutely no interest in getting caught up in things. I began to retreat slowly out of the vicinity of the deadly showdown-to-be.

"Please, Mister Feltis," the priest appealed, "let's not fight, hm? I've come here for a reason, and it's certainly not to kill you."

"Speak for yourself," Feltis growled. "I've been waiting for this, you bastard! Your spells won't work on the likes of me!"

"Mmm," the priest hummed. "I suppose if you feel that strongly, then you leave me no choice." He began casting a spell, the calm smile never leaving his face.

I could hear his incantation. As spells go, it had an odd beginning.

"Oh, no you don't!" Feltis roared. In the blink of an eye, he was upon the priest and slashing down with his long sword.

CLANG!

The beast-man was thrown back from the priest and sent tumbling through the brush.

"Wha—?!" was my immediate and less-than-insightful response. Feltis had been blown back by nothing more than the spell's *magic field*.

See, when a spell's being cast, a magic wall (sort of like a force field) surrounds the caster. The wall is generally stronger for stronger attack spells, but only to a point; to give you an idea, the Dragon Slave, said to be the most powerful attack spell, provides a wall that still can't withstand a third-rate sorcerer's fireball or a first-rate swordsman's slashes.

Until right then, I'd never seen an attacker—especially one as powerful-looking as Feltis—deflected by a magic field alone. What the hell was that priest chanting?

"W-what happened?!" Feltis stammered as he staggered to his feet. As he did so, the priest delicately pointed a finger at him and released the Power Words.

"Blast Bomb!"

As the air whooshed and whined, dozens of balls of light sprung forth around the priest. Then they tore through the air, spiraling to converge directly where he pointed.

That's when my inner voice gave me a simple and desperate instruction: *Duck!*

I hit the ground as the balls of light slammed into the very unlucky Feltis.

KA-BOOOOOOOOM!

The massive roar was followed by a concussive shockwave and, finally, by a blast of overheated air. The hands I slapped over my ears barely managed to keep my eardrums from bursting.

"Nngh!" I grunted, cringing tight and low to the ground. After the air quieted, I tentatively opened my eyes.

The first thing I realized was that Feltis was gone. Well, not so much *gone* as reduced to a smattering of orange-colored powder. That was an eerie sign that he'd been vaporized—a sign scattered all over the bushes and twigs near where he'd been standing.

I considered that maybe he'd escaped and the dust was just cumin, but that was probably just my humane side talking. *Pretty impressive firepower for your average priest*, I thought, then suddenly stopped.

Balgumon and Amelia were gone!

For a second, I panicked and thought they'd gotten in the path of the attack. A sudden horrifying mental image of me delivering a box of paprika with my condolences to Phil crossed my mind. Once I thought for a moment, though, I doubted they'd been hit directly. They'd probably just been swept away by the blast.

"My, my," the priest said clicking his tongue, like a waiter had goofed up his order of scrambled eggs. "It seems the other one got away."

His tone was more amused than agitated. He scratched his head, his face skewed into mild perplexity.

I think I've met my first sociopath.

"Mm . . . just as well," he murmured as he turned to glance in my direction. He brightened.

"Excuse me!" he called politely. "I realize this is an awkward question, but do you happen to know where that group from before congregates?"

I admit it—the man creeped me out. Doing that much damage while smiling a happy li'l smile made me think he was some sort of runaway nutcase. Then it suddenly occurred to me, like a lighting spell flicking on in my brain, just who he might be.

"Hey," I said, looking curiously at the priest. "Y-you're Rei Magnus, aren't you?!"

The priest literally fell over. Surprise can do that to some people.

"W-where in the world," he asked slowly, "did you get an idea like that?" He used his staff to prop himself back up.

"There's only one person I know of who can use the Blast Bomb, and that's Rei Magnus. That makes you him!"

"I see," the priest replied. "But Rei Magnus was a sorcerer who lived five thousand years ago, you realize."

"Details, shmetails," I scoffed. "What's a millennium or two among sorcerers? You can live as long as you want if you've got the guts!"

"And what sort of life-extending magic guts might those be?" he asked, his brows raised whimsically. "In any case, I already have a perfectly good name. I am Xelloss."

Xelloss? Never heard of you.

"Hunh." I pondered his answer. "And exactly what are you?"

"A mysterious priest," he replied cryptically without missing a beat.

I paused. That was a weird thing to say. "And what's Feltis and his group to you?"

"They're my enemies."

He wasn't giving me much to work with. He must've sensed my skepticism, because he smiled again.

"You don't trust me?" he asked.

"Being the enemy of my enemy doesn't make you my ally."

"Well . . ." Xelloss shrugged. "That's certainly true."

"Besides," I went on, "I haven't trusted priests for a while now. Long story."

Xelloss looked me over. "You do seem the 'long story' type."

Okay, let's not get smarmy.

"Anyway," I said sharply, "besides all that, I wanna know about those amulets you're wearing. They're talismans, aren't they?"

"What do you mean?" Xelloss asked, feigning ignorance.

"Those," I insisted, pointing at them. "That gem hanging from your neck, and the one on your belt buckle, and the two in your bracelets. You're using all four of them as capacity amplifiers, aren't you?"

"My," Xelloss drawled, "you've got quite the sharp eye." He actually seemed impressed, and he had shed the holier-than-thou attitude just the slightest bit, which was nice.

Sorcerers have been researching capacity amplifiers for ages, but I'd never heard of anyone successfully applying the concept. I'd researched them myself, but all I'd come up with was that amplifiers could theoretically work with the simplest of spells. Something told me Xelloss didn't need help with *those*.

But since he was playing dumb, I decided to press the case. "You cast a short spell," I said, "just before you started the Blast Bomb. I'm pretty sure the short spell was for magic amplification, but if it was that easy to make a capacity amplifier, every sage in the world wouldn't be going nuts trying to do it. In other words, that spell was caused by something else."

Xelloss smiled. "Is that why you think these are talismans?"

"Yeah. So what are they made of? They can't be normal jewels."

Xelloss cocked his head as he pondered my question. "Honestly," he said, "I'm not really sure. They were gifts, you see." As he looked at me with that pleasant expression on his face, I wondered if he had a brain inside that skull.

Speaking of empty skulls, I suddenly remembered Gourry. I hoped he was all right.

Xelloss glanced at the talismans. "They're supposedly Demon Bloodstones. Ruby Eye, Dark Star, Chaotic Blue, and Death Fog—from the Demon Lord of this world, and three Demon Lords of other worlds."

That was enough to blow anyone's mind, even a mind as sharp as mine.

"D-Demon Lords of *other worlds?!*" I stuttered. My jaw dropped and my eyes bugged out of my head. "No way! Is that really true?!"

"I'm not sure," Xelloss repeated. "That's what they tell me."

"Who?" I asked quickly, feeling like a startled owl. "Who tells you?"

"It's a s-e-c-r-e-t," he calmly replied, wagging his finger at me.

I scowled. *Don't make me smack the smart out of you, jerky.*

"Well, they're definitely unique, whatever they are." A thought suddenly hit me; I clasped my hands together.

"That's it!" I exclaimed. "You should sell them to me!"

Xelloss blinked. "Why in the world would I do a thing like that?" he asked in response to my excellent idea.

"Because I want them, duh. Look—I'll pay you five hundred and fifty for them. I mean, seriously, that's an awesome price! Aren't I generous? You could buy yourself a *rapier* with that kind of money!"

Xelloss just laughed. "Five hundred and fifty *thousand* and they're yours."

Without hesitating, I shot back, "Sold!"

"Huh?" Xelloss froze, and I swear the word JACKASS appeared over his head in neon lights.

"You said you'd sell them for five hundred and fifty thousand, right?" I grabbed the sack from my back, unfurled it, and began taking various magical items out.

"Let's see," I mused aloud. "One bundle of crowley roots, two meltian medicines, one radilin ring, remtite ore, five bags of mustaal powder . . . oh, and what the hell, I'll even throw in a crufer pill! At any major city," I explained, squinting my eyes and pinching my fingers like a shrewd merchant, "you could sell these for well over five hundred and fifty thousand, no question. It seems we've got ourselves a deal."

But Xelloss just started gibbering. "Oh . . . um . . . well . . ."

"Don't tell me you don't wanna sell after we agreed on a price fair and square." I gave Xelloss a stare that stabbed right through his pupils.

"But . . . um . . ."

STAB.

Finally, his eyes lowered and his shoulders drooped. "Yes, ma'am," he murmured.

Score!

With a resigned sigh, Xelloss removed the four talismans and reluctantly handed them over.

"You may as well know," he told me, "that to use the amplifiers, hold them in front of you in a cross posture while chanting the Amplification spell before the spell you wish to use. As for the Amplification spell—"

"That's fine," I cut in, waving him off. "I already heard you chant it. I'll take it from here."

"Huh?" Xelloss blurted. He made a little cooing noise in his throat. I think I impressed him.

I have that effect on men, ya see.

"That's really something," he said. "Remembering a spell you've only heard once, even if it *is* a short one."

"I guess," I replied somewhat cockily. Then, just so I didn't seem too cocky, I added, "I did a little research into this stuff awhile back."

I put the talismans on. They may not have worked for me fashion-wise, but with power comes sacrifice.

"Research?" Xelloss asked. "Does that mean you're a sorceress?"

I raised an eyebrow. "The outfit didn't tip you off?"

Xelloss shrugged. "I thought maybe you were just eccentric. Or playing dress-up."

"Hey!"

"Okay, okay." Xelloss held out his hands as if to apologize. "But you didn't use any magic in the battle earlier. Was there a particular reason for that?"

I winced. *Way to hit me when I'm down,* I wanted to tell him, although I wasn't sure I wanted to share the ugly truth at all. After thinking a second, I figured it wasn't going to change much.

"My spells," I said with a sigh, "got sealed."

Xelloss delicately gripped his chin. "So there's someone here with the power to do that, is there?"

"Yeah," I mumbled. "She's part of the jerk squad. Calls herself Mazenda."

Xelloss looked at me like I'd just sprouted three heads. "Ehhhhhhhhhhhh?!" he cried, taking two staggering steps back. "Miss Mazenda's one of them?!"

"W-wait a minute!" I shook my head and waved at him to calm down. "You mean you know her?!" Surprises were flying fast and furious that day.

Xelloss straightened himself with his staff. He paused a moment, then scratched his head.

"Well, sort of," he explained. "But right now, it seems that we're enemies."

Did he say seems? "I'm sensing complications."

"Indeed." Xelloss glanced around, then added, "But this isn't a very good place for conversation." He dumped the items I'd given him into a satchel. "Why don't we go to the nearest village and continue this there?"

"Great," I replied as I rubbed my stomach appreciatively. "All this talk is making me hungry."

***

The closest village had a decent tavern, so we went and grabbed some breakfast. It was around noon by the time we finished, so the morning crowd had gone and the lunch-goers were still at their day jobs. For the moment, we had the place almost to ourselves.

"That's quite a fix you've gotten yourself into," Xelloss commented as he looked into his hot milk. "If the story you just told me is true, of course."

I nodded and went back to sipping my tea. "Truth is stranger than fiction, they always say."

"But if your spells are sealed," Xelloss said, "doesn't that make buying my talismans rather meaningless?"

"No," I answered flatly. *You're not buying them back, if that's what you mean.* "Once a day I've tried to cast a lighting

77

spell, and the good news is that the seal seems to be getting weaker. The bad news is that a candle-level light's not gonna do much in a fight." I slumped back in my chair and glanced at my new acquisitions, stowed away in my bag. "I figure that with those talismans, I might be able to handle some basic attack spells."

"I see," Xelloss said with a nod. "But for the seal to be breaking down like this . . ." He shook his head. "Either Miss Mazenda went easy on you, or your magic capacity is unusually large."

Both, I hoped.

"Whatever it is," I said, "my main concern right now is finding Gourry." I paused a second, then frowned. "Well, maybe Gourry can fend for himself; I should probably worry more about Amelia."

Xelloss waved his hand in a dismissive gesture. "I'm sure she's fine."

I glared at him. "And what makes you so sure of that, Mister Omniscient?"

He took a sip of his hot milk. "When you faced Feltis and Balgumon this morning, they could have easily disposed of Miss Amelia on the spot, correct?"

I nodded slowly, putting together the pieces of what Xelloss had said.

"If we assume he fled after the Blast Bomb," Xelloss continued, "and that, since we didn't find either of them, he took her with him, he must have some purpose for her. After all, a hostage slows a retreat; you don't take one unless you need one."

"So he wants to use her as bait. To get me."

Xelloss nodded over his milk.

I tilted my head as far back as it could go and sighed. "I could've told you that," I muttered. "Use her to lure me to them? That's the oldest trick in the book. But at least that means she's safe for the moment."

"Since Miss Mazenda is with the enemy," he added, "they may have sealed Amelia's magic to keep her cooperative. It's far less painful than, say, crushing her windpipe."

Xelloss looked away, mulling the situation over. "Furthermore, should you decide to attack them, they can use Miss Amelia as a shield. Though I'm sure they'd rather dispose of her *after* defeating you; it's logical to assume that they're planning to sacrifice her."

I almost choked on my tea. "S-sacrifice?!" I blurted.

"Mmm," Xelloss replied, perfectly composed. "The enemy is a religious organization, after all. You know how extreme religions are quite fond of elaborate sacrifices to their gods. And they worship quite a god, don't they? The Demon Lord himself!" Xelloss leaned forward, resting his arms on the table and clasping his fingers together. "It doesn't take much to see what I'm getting at."

"Are you talking about a *human* sacrifice?!" I squeaked, my voice tiny in my throat.

"Precisely. In theory, a human sacrifice should be young and beautiful. I sincerely doubt they'd harm and potentially waste a captive who fit that profile."

Xelloss smiled wryly, but behind his eyes I sensed bitterness. "Though I suppose," he said quietly, "humans who happily worship Mazoku are capable of anything."

I pushed away my tea. "Well, a lot of people will have their fun so long as somebody else picks up the tab. If the righteous gods won't grant you your selfish desires, why not turn to worshipping the Demon Lord instead?"

"Why not indeed," Xelloss answered solemnly.

"But there's always the chance she's *just* bait. How sure are you about the sacrifice thing?"

"Quite sure," Xelloss replied. "Master Krotz is thoroughly pragmatic."

"Krotz?" I repeated. The name sounded familiar.

"He's their leader. Or their founder, if you will."

Oh. Right.

It was the name Balgumon had mentioned at the assembly the other night. Talking about what the cult intended to do with

Amelia was getting a bit too creepy, though. I decided to turn my attention to Xelloss and put him in the hot seat for a minute.

"So," I said, staring straight at him. "What business do *you* have with that nasty little mob?"

"I had a tussle with them near Raizeel." He paused, then took a breath. "To make a long story short, Master Krotz stole an object of mine and brought it back here, to his stronghold."

Well, I'll give him points for brevity.

"That was an impressively short summary," I quipped, but I wasn't done grilling him yet. "What's this so-called 'object' he stole?"

Xelloss smiled. "It's not much of anything, really," he said, but he was lying. It was easy to tell from the way he averted his gaze and took an exaggeratedly long slurp of his milk.

"Hang on," I snapped. "You can't tell me it's some unimportant doodad after I saw you vaporize Feltis. Spit it out."

Xelloss mumbled some more, but it was obvious I was wearing him down. "Er . . . um . . ." He leaned forward and said quietly, "Just a manuscript. Nothing special."

Manuscript? What kind of—wait. It's not . . . it couldn't be . . . Lina, don't get excited!

"No way!" I blurted and shot out of my seat like my butt was on fire.

"Miss Lina!" Xelloss suddenly looked unnerved. "Not so loud!"

I took a second to pull myself together, and shakily sat back down. As Xelloss nervously cleared his throat, I noticed the tavernkeeper giving us a shifty, suspicious gaze from the other side of the room.

I leaned in. "Manuscript?" I asked in a low, harsh whisper. "You mean, *that* manuscript?"

Xelloss frowned. "Well, perhaps. If we're talking about the same manuscript."

I took a deep breath. "The Claire Bible?" Just the name sent a shiver through me.

Xelloss nodded curtly.

***

The Claire Bible is a magic book, a legend among sorcerers, the very book in which Mazoku record their secrets of sorcery. It's an ancient tome and an absolute one-of-a-kind, though a number of incomplete copies exist in various places; in sorcerer-talk, those portions are referred to as "manuscripts." In spite of strong evidence, there are even some who refuse to believe the Claire Bible actually exists, but I happened to know it *did*.

Awhile back, my big sis from the countryside and I went on a trip to the Kingdom of Dils. While there, we heard a legend about a manuscript that was once kept in the royal palace, at least until someone—some absolute numbskull if you ask me—burned it. Fortunately, the contents of the manuscript survived, and I was lucky enough to hear some of those sacred contents recited while I was there. A lot of it was a load of crap, but on a lark I tried combining two of the spells I heard.

And got the Giga Slave.

You know, the spell that draws on the power of the Demon Lord of Demon Lords, the Lord of Nightmares? The spell that brings a great void into the world? That one.

Giga Slave's destructive power is well beyond even that of the Dragon Slave, which is supposedly the most powerful spell a human can wield. The fact that the Giga Slave worked proved the Claire Bible's existence. But I never reported my discovery to the Sorcerers' Guild.

Still, there were so many fake manuscripts floating around that the one Xelloss and the cult fought over could have easily been a dud. I had to consider it.

"This 'manuscript,' " I asked him, tapping a finger on the table for emphasis. "Is it the real deal? There are lots of villages that say they have authentic manuscripts just to boost tourism."

"Ah," Xelloss uttered, nodding. "There are plenty of fakes, I'll give you that. Many a casual collector will spend a fortune on a tome labeled *The Legendary Magic Book* and not bother to notice it's an ancient book of cake mixes." He drew closer to me and whispered, "But I'm sure about this one. It's most certainly real."

Xelloss paused for me to take in the certainty of his claim. "I admit," he added, "that I'm only going on intuition. But for Master Krotz to seize the manuscript with a force of half his followers, and then place it solely in his care while transporting it back to his stronghold . . ." He smiled. "He must feel very strongly about its authenticity."

Xelloss's logic felt a bit strained, but I was willing to let it slide. There was a more important question to get to.

"All right," I began, leveling a steely gaze at him. "Then what are the contents of this manuscript? And more important, what are you gonna do with it if you get it?"

Xelloss paused. "Well," he said at last, looking a bit perplexed, "there are various circumstances on my side related to that. And I'm afraid there are things I can say and things I cannot.

"However," he offered, "I can promise you this: I absolutely will not use the manuscript for evil purposes."

I rolled my eyes. *How many times have I heard that one?*

I obviously wasn't about to swallow his righteous act and make him godfather of my kids, but at least he seemed genuinely opposed to Krotz and his demon-worshipping cronies. With Gourry MIA and my magic weak and unreliable, I needed Xelloss as an ally, if only temporarily.

"Fine," I said, as diplomatically as I could. "I won't push it. But what the hell do Krotz and his people want the manuscript for?"

Xelloss smiled at my question—a dark, acidic little smile.

"Asking me that," he said softly, "puts me on the spot, I'm afraid. But this religious organization probably doesn't have the well-being of the world's population high on its list of objectives, wouldn't you say?"

It wasn't much of an answer, but he had a point. "Fine," I replied, and that brought me to *my* point. "Can I make a suggestion?"

"I'm guessing you'd like to join forces with me for a bit."

He's not as idiotic as his smiles; I'll give him that.

"You got it. I don't know where the cult's stronghold is, but I can lead you to their meeting place; it's not far from here. And knowing I have an ally right now will help me sleep a little easier."

"Very well." Xelloss nodded. "And with Miss Mazenda among the enemy, we can't possibly ignore them."

"There's a special problem with her, I take it?"

Xelloss put his finger to his lips. "It's a secret."

I was going to come to hate that line.

***

By late evening, I was absolutely exhausted. I used an alias to secure lodging at a nearby inn, and by the time I managed to drag myself up the stairs to my room, I was barely able to pull off my boots before collapsing into bed.

Unfortunately, my enemies didn't feel like allowing me the twelve or more hours of sleep I felt entitled to. I was suddenly jolted awake by a burning bloodlust nearby—*burning*, as you'll soon see, being the operative word.

What the hell is going on?!

In the darkness, I snatched up my sword and reached for the mantle lying across a corner of my bed. Then, just at that moment:

FWOOSH!

A stupendous shockwave almost flung me off the bed as I donned my mantle. Jumping to my feet, I bolted for the door and pulled it open.

I recoiled from the intense heat and the acrid smell of burning wood. As I staggered, another tremor shook the inn as an explosion tore into the building from somewhere nearby. It felt like the whole joint was going to fall right off its foundations. Another explosion jacked up the heat another notch, and from the hallway I saw the stairway suffused in an ominous orange glow. It was clear to my finely tuned senses that that was a sign to *keep the hell away!*

Someone was attacking the inn—that much was abundantly clear. And who were they after, you ask?

Everyone's favorite target: me. And maybe Xelloss, considering the circumstances.

I ran back into my room, cast a levitation spell, and jumped out the window . . .

. . . completely forgetting about my magic being sealed.

CRASH! Thwack-thwack-thwack CRUNCH!

"Owowowow!"

I had managed to float for about half a second before my weakened powers gave out. Luckily, there was a tree outside my window and hitting the branches slowed my fall enough that I escaped with no more than some scratches and bruised pride.

And, stupid me, I forgot about using the talismans, too.

With some effort and a lot of cursing, I managed to extricate myself from the low-lying tangle of branches. As I jumped to the ground, pulling twigs and leaves from my hair, I noticed the last person I wanted to see standing not far away.

"It's been awhile," Mazenda drawled in her condescending tone. A hint of a smile curved her red lips. "Balgumon told me who you are. You're *the* Lina Inverse?"

She took a step closer to me. In the light of the flames that consumed the inn, I could see the glimmer of evil in her eyes.

"A-Amelia," I managed to stutter. "Are Amelia and Gourry all right?" As she took another step, I retreated instinctively from the overpowering and unpleasant aura the woman gave off. The sweat streaking down my forehead wasn't just because of the fire; Mazenda herself made me extremely nervous.

"Ah, the girl is all right," Mazenda purred. "At least, she should be. I don't know about the other one."

"What did the beast-man tell you?" I demanded, trying to sound as plucky as I could. "Vedur, or whatever his name is."

Mazenda's ruby locks tossed in the hot wind like flickering tongues of flame. She took another step forward; I took another back.

"I haven't spoken with *him*," she said dismissively. "Only with Balgumon. I admit I was surprised to learn who you are. If I'd known that you were Lina Inverse, I would've killed you during our first encounter instead of toying with you like this."

"You think it was smart to set fire to an entire inn just to get to me? You're not very subtle, are you?" I held my ground. "Or maybe you're just stupid."

At least if she kills me now, I managed to insult her first.

A thoughtful expression came over Mazenda's face. "Actually," she said, more seriously, "Balgumon also told me there was someone else with you. A mysterious priest, was it?" She chuckled unpleasantly. "But I fear I won't have the pleasure of meeting him. He's nothing but cinders now."

"Not quite," I said, staring past her. "Look behind you."

Mazenda burst out laughing. "Do you really expect me to fall for that pathetic trick?" she asked. "Please!"

"Behind you, Miss Mazenda."

Upon hearing his voice, the smile dropped from Mazenda's lips and an expression of alarm froze her face. "It . . . it can't be," she breathed.

Slowly, she turned her head. It didn't take long for her to notice the black-robed priest standing behind her.

"Xelloss!" she shrieked. "W-what are *you* doing here?!"

"I ought to ask you the same thing," Xelloss said with a pained smile. "I never dreamed I'd find you an active member of a Demon Lord cult." He took a deep, thoughtful breath. "But, since we're here, you do know what your founder is up to, don't you? What he's returning with?"

Mazenda's eyes grew wide. "You mean Krotz actually has it? He's coming back with . . ." Her quivering voice trailed off as the shock overwhelmed her.

"Yes." Xelloss bobbed his head. "The Claire Bible." After a pause, he continued in a quieter tone, "You and I are enemies because of this. Even if we weren't, I couldn't let you get away with stealing my manuscript, now could I?"

"W-what do you intend to do?" Mazenda asked feebly as she stepped back. I was glad to see her cut down to size; this woman, who just minutes ago had been able to terrorize me with her aura alone, had been reduced to a sniveling weasel.

Xelloss laughed. "As if there was any doubt." The smile on his face pitilessly mocked Mazenda's fear.

"N-no!" Mazenda shrieked. She suddenly turned, ran toward the fiery inn, and plunged into the raging inferno through a broken window.

And that, ladies and gentlemen, is *fear*.

"Hey!" I cried, lurching forward. As I did, Xelloss gently placed a hand on my shoulder.

"Xelloss!" I yelled angrily. "What the hell's going on here?!"

Xelloss didn't answer my question. He just kept his eyes fixed on the walls of flames before him.

"I'm going to follow her," he said after a moment.

"What?! Into the fire?!"

"For now, yes."

"Are you nuts?!" Xelloss was losing it. Well, if he'd ever had it to begin with. "She's gotta be burned to a crisp by now!"

"No, it's all right. This fire isn't enough to kill her."

Well, hell. Sorry, Xelloss—my mistake.

"In any case," he added, straightening himself, "I'll be following her from now on. I'll manage somehow."

"I repeat: are you out of your mind? What do you mean 'somehow'?!"

"Meaning, that I'll free your spells up eventually. So please don't worry." From the look on his face, he seemed to be the calmest, most determined guy I'd ever met considering what he was quite literally about to jump into.

Xelloss placed a hand on my shoulder. "I apologize for breaking up our partnership so soon after we formed it, but I absolutely must go. Now, can you give me any hint as to where that stronghold might be?"

"Uh, Mane," I blurted. "It's somewhere around there."

"Thank you. We shall meet again soon." With that, he walked up to the fiery inn, smiled back at me once, and then leapt through the window and into the flames.

I stood a safe distance away and watched the fire consume the building for the next several minutes. Try as I might, I could see nothing moving inside the crackling flames.

"What the hell just happened here?" I muttered to myself. In the back of my mind, a funny thought occurred to me: what if, in the morning, I came back to find two bodies charred to a crisp in the ruins of the inn?

Okay, maybe not funny so much as gross and disturbing.

***

The next day, I decided to head straight for Mane Village. After splitting from Xelloss the night before—or, I should say, after him leaving me to rush suicidally into a burning building—I decided it might be best if I disguised myself before continuing.

I've never been one for complicated disguises. Usually, I just wear ordinary village girl's clothes, braid my hair, and try to look harmless. This almost always works, because most of the people I have to hide from are very, very stupid.

This situation was no exception. As long as I didn't run into Vedur or Balgumon, I doubted any of the cult's goons had the mental capacity to blow my cover. After all, most of my pursuers had no clue what I looked like—just that I was a tough-looking sorceress about fifteen or sixteen years old. As long as I looked like a wimpy, ordinary girl, I could easily fool the lot of them.

If only I was better at acting girly, I'd be all set!

I've never been the type to wear skirts and dressy shoes and all that impractical feminine junk, so my awkward gait probably drew more attention than I intended. Seriously, though, I knew that once I got the walk down, it'd be a great disguise.

My plan of action was to first find Gourry, then retrieve my spells with Xelloss' covert help, and, if my luck held out, meet up with Xelloss once I got to Mane. The problem with this plan was that it assumed that nothing unexpected would occur in the short term, which has never happened. Ever.

Oh, and a few tests before leaving proved that I could cast a fireball-level spell if I used the talismans and Amplification. I still only had the power of a rookie sorcerer, but it was better than nothing.

"Hey, you! Woman!"

The man's voice that interrupted my planning sounded annoyed.

"Come over here," it ordered from the roadside.

I turned in his direction and affected a startled look. "Come over there? W-Why?"

The group of thugs that emerged from the woods consisted of five men, all of them masked. It wasn't surprising; I'd expected to run into cult goons at some point, and I could take on five opponents even without my spells.

But what made me hesitate was the thought of Vedur, the beast-man, and how I'd have to deal with him once word about me got out. Vedur wasn't someone to mess with when you weren't at full power.

"Who the hell're you?" the man asked. "And where're you going?"

Time to bluff my way out of this. I swallowed my pride and pretended to shiver and wince nervously at his questions. The man doing the talking held a long sword, and I didn't want to get any closer to it.

"I-I-I'm . . . Lily," I stammered. "I'm taking a package for someone in Saillune."

"Huh," the man huffed. He looked me over from head to toe in a way that seriously tested my restraint; I would've liked nothing more than to punch his ugly face in. As he checked me out, one of his flunkies glared at me and said: "Have I seen you somewhere before?"

THUMP.

My heart skipped a beat. Had he been in the gang that had ambushed me earlier?

"Heh," he cackled, "maybe we oughta do a full body search. Don't ya think?"

Oh. For a second there I actually thought he was thinking with his brain.

The doofus didn't actually remember me, he was just fishing for an excuse to peek at a seemingly helpless girl. Disgusting letch! I tried to remember his face so I could kill him later.

Unfortunately, the pack on my back held my mantle, clothing, and all my magic items, and I'd stashed my sword and its sheath under my clothes. My cover would get blown the second anyone opened my pack.

Time for a new plan.

"Hmph!" I huffed with a sneer. "I'm definitely not impressed." I laughed in a way that I hoped was both condescending and dainty.

"Hey!" the first man growled. "What's with the attitude, slut?!"

Now, normally, I'd have reacted to anyone talking to me like that with a swift kick to the squish. But I managed to stay composed and in character.

"If you're all Mazenda's got, I can understand why she called *me* here."

"Wha—?" the man blurted, not sure whether to be angry or embarrassed. Mentioning Mazenda by name had certainly caught them off-guard. "Just what the hell do you mean by that?"

"What do you think I mean? Mazenda and I go way back. She sent me a message informing me of a situation, and asked for my help on the matter. So here I am."

The men spoke briefly among themselves. The first of them to break from the huddle asked me, "Really?"

"If you don't believe me," I said sharply, "then I'll be on my way home." I turned on my heels and began briskly walking back in the direction I'd come from.

"I do hope Mazenda won't be too upset," I called over my shoulder. "Have fun explaining the situation to her when you see her."

"W-wait!" The man abruptly ran after me; I found the sudden desperation in his voice pretty funny. "If you're on the level, then we'd better let you through or she's gonna kill us!"

The other men voiced their firm agreement.

"But if it turns out you're bluffin', then look out."

I shrugged nonchalantly. "So why don't you just go ask Mazenda herself?"

"Er . . . uh . . ." he stuttered. I sighed impatiently.

This is really getting tiresome.

"All right, all right," I interjected. "I'll make a deal with you. I'll go as far as Mane and lodge at an inn. When you report to Mazenda, tell her that Melty's waiting for her at the inn."

The masked men again had a quick discussion among themselves.

"Hey!" the first man suddenly yelled. "I thought you said your name was Lily!"

Dammit, Lina, it would help if you could get your fake names straight!

"I was lying to you, of course." My insides shook with fear, but I somehow managed to sound calm. "I was just testing to see how perceptive you were."

"Is that right?" the first man guffawed, pleased with himself.

That's why I like third-rate villains—so gullible.

"Miss," another asked, "why don't we escort you as far as Mane?"

I waved off that suggestion just as lightly. "If you do that much for a common traveler, it'll only look suspicious. You might be better guards if you stopped making stupid suggestions." With that, I began traipsing away. And in a very convincing girlish fashion, I might add.

"Don't forget to give Mazenda my message, boys," I twittered back at them, waving goodbye.

Oh, Lina, how can you be so smart?

***

The rest of the journey was uneventful, so I put my original plan into action as soon as I reached the village. There was no sign of Gourry or Xelloss there. I had hoped, at least, that I might meet up with Xelloss, but it was clear from the fact that my magic powers were still sealed that he was busy with his own mission. That also meant that Mazenda was still alive. I hoped, at least, that she hadn't killed Xelloss and left me *completely* screwed.

On the one hand, I was glad I'd managed to get into Mane—enemy territory, practically. But now that I was there, what was I supposed to do? I had no leads, no resources, and no effective way to attack my enemies.

I'm not one to sit around and sulk, though, or give up and rot away in my room. I'm Lina Inverse, woman of action, sorceress extraordinaire, and I never accept defeat!

So, off I went.

***

"My brothers!" Krotz boomed, his voice resounding in the darkness.

You guessed it. I'd snuck back into the cult's meeting place, the ruins of the coliseum hidden away in the mountains near Mane.

It had been five days since I'd arrived in Mane, and every one of those five nights I'd ventured up to the coliseum in the hopes of catching another of the cult's secret meetings. So far, I'd had no luck, but on the fifth night, it was showtime again. My method of sneaking in was the same: I hid on the coliseum's uppermost tier, where I had the least chance of being seen. Getting up there wasn't a problem, since I could at least handle a levitation spell with a little help from the talismans' amplification powers.

My objective this time wasn't to crash the meeting but to see if I could catch wind of where the group's headquarters were. Sneaking in by myself with my powers compromised was a risky stunt, but it was either that or twiddling my thumbs back at my lodgings while I waited for Gourry or Xelloss to show up. Like I said, that's just not my style.

As I peered over the ledge, I noticed that the guy addressing the congregation wasn't Balgumon. This guy was much younger, with a head of dark hair and a slender face. If I didn't hate his guts by default, I might've even thought of him as handsome. Even from way above, where I crouched, I noticed a glint in his eyes and a charisma in his voice and style; in short, he was everything that pipsqueak Balgumon wasn't.

The speaker wore a flowing black robe that flapped around him as he exhorted the crowds and gestured passionately with his hands. Then, during a pause in his speech, he lowered his arms and let them rest at this sides.

"Be pleased," he boomed. "That which we desire is now within our grasp!"

With that, a huge roar of delight reverberated throughout the congregation. It practically made the stars shudder.

"Yes," he continued, "true power, true *terror* is finally within my grasp! Now the fools who worship the gods shall know their heresy, *for we have the power!*"

Once more, the coliseum shook, this time even more thunderously with the cheers and applause of the adoring crowd. They were obviously mesmerized by every word this guy—who could only be Krotz—uttered.

"First," Krotz said, "Saillune!"

I found my interest immediately piqued by the mention of Saillune.

Hasn't that city been through enough already?

"They have the audacity to call their city the Holy Capital, a city of White Magic that worships Ceiphied!" Krotz sneered bombastically. "By destroying it first, the entire world shall know our might!"

My eyes went wide.

Wait a minute! Destroy it?!

The guy either suffered from a screwed-up sense of humor or was even loonier than I thought.

Now, I get that exaggeration is an essential part of any organization's rhetoric, especially one as foul and twisted as the Cult of Shabranigdu. But you'd expect even the most zealous of leaders to backtrack a little after making a whopper of a claim like that. Something like, "Heh heh, I was just kidding. We can't actually do that."

Suddenly, a sickening realization dawned on me.

They *could* do it. Destroy Saillune, using the manuscript.

Still, even if they did have that kind of power, it was hard for me to believe that anybody would actually use it. That is, until I remembered that the guy making the claims was a megalomaniacal cult leader who suddenly had more power than pretty much anyone and consistently showed signs of being really, *really* insane.

All of a sudden, things aren't looking too good for the world.

"Several days ago," Krotz went on, changing the topic, "a band of outlaws disrupted our assembly here." An angry murmur rippled through the crowd, but Krotz quickly quieted them with a gesture. "You need not be concerned!" he assured them. "One of them has been captured by our comrade Bishop Balgumon, and the other two shall soon fall into our hands."

I breathed a small sigh of relief after hearing that; it meant that Gourry hadn't been captured yet and was most likely still alive.

That was all the important stuff covered at the meeting. The rest was just Krotz yammering on and on about justice, the nature of evil, and the true nature of mankind, blah, blah, blah.

After he finally finished his pep talk/sermon/warmongering diatribe, the assembled cult members chanted a spell in unison, appealing to Ruby Eye for his "glorious" grace. And on that cheery note, the meeting concluded.

Krotz and his entourage made their exit from the coliseum, each torch on their route flickering out as they left. The congregation also made to leave, but less impressively: they thronged the exits, talked among themselves, and waited to be let through.

It's now or never.

Using Levitation under the cover of darkness, I descended to the floor of the coliseum and joined the crowd of cult members. I was in disguise, of course—I'd changed into men's clothing and put on a mask like the ones the cult members wore. I couldn't disguise my voice, but as far as appearance was concerned I could easily pass for some kid brought along by his bad role-model father. Sometimes, I had to admit, being short and not having the most ample breasts in the world did have its advantages.

Given a choice, though, I'd definitely take the extra height and curves, and give up being able to pass for a prepubescent boy.

In any case, there I was, a part of the stream of cult followers slowly filing out the exit. My objective was to get a lead on Krotz, because if anyone was heading for the cult's super-secret headquarters, it was him.

Unfortunately, I was completely unarmed. A sword would've drawn too much attention, so I'd left mine back in Mane Village with the rest of my belongings. The talismans, though, I couldn't do without. I'd hidden them under my disguise: large bracelets concealed the amulets on my wrists and a scarf tied around my throat hid the talisman-bearing necklace. The belt-buckle talisman I wore under my clothes. Okay, so maybe the bracelets and scarf were a little odd considering I was supposed to be a man, but it was the best I could come up with under the circumstances.

It helped that the cult's security was amazingly crappy. Not only was it way too easy to spy on their entire secret meeting, but going unnoticed while standing right in a crowd of them turned out to be even easier. For a moment I thought I might actually find their headquarters without a hitch.

Yeah, that was a nice thought. As usual, it didn't last.

What I hadn't counted on was the fact that the cult was actually hyper-organized in a way I hadn't guessed. As I got closer to the exit, I noticed that instead of leaving randomly (like you'd expect from a group of this size), the cult members seemed to have very specific routes planned, along very specific paths, and none of them moved alone. Worst of all were the men in red mantles and masks up ahead, paying close attention and making sure that everybody was where they were supposed to be. Far from having lax security, I realized now that it didn't matter to them who spied on their meeting, because they were sure to catch the spy on the way out.

There's no turning back now. Think, Lina!

For the time being, I followed along with the general group as it made its way out of the meeting hall. A large number of the believers took up torches and began heading back toward the village, so I hid among them and hoped I'd get overlooked. The moment it seemed no one was watching, I dove out of the line, hid myself in the underbrush, and waited for the group to pass.

So far, so good.

By the time I'd picked my way back to the coliseum, the last stragglers from the meeting were gone. I hid in the brush for a while, occasionally checking for any signs of movement or activity.

Then, I lucked out. I heard movement not far from where I hid.

Several silhouettes appeared at a small opening not far from the exit the congregation had used. There were about ten guys, some holding staves with lighting spells illuminating the tips. One of the staff-bearers, his face glowing faintly in the light, was Krotz. The group took a path that led them away from the village and deeper into the mountains.

Now we're getting somewhere!

I began to follow the trail of lights. The path was rocky and uneven, and I couldn't use any light of my own and still remain undetected. I somehow managed to trail them without falling or tripping or otherwise making loud noises that would give me away. If I had been caught, even in my mask and disguise, I would've had a hard time explaining just what the hell I was doing following their secret procession to their secret temple.

As I snuck along, I suddenly got the freaky sensation that *I* was being followed. Was there someone on the path behind me? Swallowing my panic, I tried to weigh my options.

Options? What options?

Turning around to face whoever it was would be tantamount to saying, "Hi, I'm your enemy!" I had no choice but to pretend not to notice.

All I could hope was for my disguise to stave off suspicion. But if it did come to a confrontation, how could I fight whoever was tailing me without sounding the alarm?

"Hey!" a firm voice called to me. "You there!"

My heart froze. The sound came not far from my right.

Time for Wimpy Kid Act Number Two.

"Y-yes?" I said, turning in the direction of the voice.

A masked figure dressed in red stood there—a muscular figure with an imposing, manly voice. Hell, saying he was muscular was an understatement. Whoever the guy was, he was built like a mountain and stood a head taller than Gourry. His voice didn't sound familiar.

"What are you doing in a place like this?" he asked.

"I-I got split off from Daddy," I whimpered. "I saw the lights up ahead and followed."

The man shook his head. "Mmmm," he sighed. "A lost kid."

Phew, I think he bought it.

"You're going the wrong way," he said. "The village is *that* way." He clicked his tongue impatiently. "Still, I can't send a kid back alone. It's dangerous out here at night."

I was about to protest with a feeble whine when he stepped toward me. "Say," he inquired gruffly, "whose boy are you?"

"Eh?" I yelped, not expecting to be interrogated at that time of night and in the middle of nowhere.

"Don't squeal like a little girl—be a man. I'm just asking you where you live and who your daddy is. I'll walk you there."

Now he wants to know who's my daddy?

It was *not* the time for an evil cult follower to get all *parental* on me! Nothing good was going to come of this, I could feel it.

I sighed moodily. "That's okay," I said, "just gimme a torch or something, and I'll get back by myself. I'm not a little kid, y'know."

"Now, hold on," the man said. "Don't give me that 'I'm not a little kid' rubbish. From the looks of it, that's *all* you are. And your voice hasn't even dropped yet." The man rocked on his heels and grunted. "As you heard at today's meeting, there's been a suspicious bunch hanging around here lately. I'm not about to let you go wandering in the dark by yourself with those hoodlums around."

So, a member of an insane death cult is calling me a suspicious hoodlum. What's wrong with this picture?

He'd been interrogating me for so long that I'd lost sight of Krotz and his entourage. Their lighted staffs had disappeared around a bend somewhere farther up the path.

If I didn't wriggle myself out of this one fast, I had no hope of catching up with them. For a second I considered just beating the guy up, leaving him a bloody heap in the forest, and going along my merry way—but without my powers, and not knowing how good the guy was in a fight, the plan was too risky. I had to keep playing along.

"Gotcha, pops," I chirped. "You can walk me to the village entrance. I'm sure you've got better things to do than gab with a little girl, er, boy like me, right?"

"Ha!" the man erupted. "You're a cheeky one, aren't you?" With that, the man chanted a small spell under his breath. A moment later, a small magic light sprung to life on the tip of his staff and spread a faint, flickering glow over the mountain trail.

"Hunh," I remarked. "You can use magic?"

"A bit." The man sniffed and thrust his chest out like he was the toughest guy on the block. "Now, let's be off."

He stopped and spun around to face me. "Oh," he added. "And you'd better take off that mask."

I'd better what?

"Eh?" I squeaked, my throat contracting with sudden panic.

"Take off the mask," he repeated. "This light may be enough to see by, but just barely. I'd rather not have you break your neck from tripping over some stray root or rock."

"W-well," I stuttered frantically, "why don't you, uh, take yours off first?" *That might hold him for a couple seconds.*

The man groaned impatiently. "Because," he muttered. "I have a somewhat frightening face."

Well, you can't say he wasn't honest.

I gathered he was another beast-man. Now that he mentioned it, I did catch a hint of a strangely shaped face protruding from under his mask.

"Now," he insisted. "Take your mask off or we won't go another step."

When I still hesitated, he grumbled and sent one of his massive hands toward me.

BOOOOOM!

Something in the distance had exploded. The night air trembled and we both gasped, whipping around to the source of the noise.

"What the hell?!" the man cried.

Up ahead in the direction that Krotz had gone, a bright flame flashed for an instant. After a moment, a thin plume of smoke rose from where the flash had been.

Somebody's firing off magic spells in the middle of nowhere. What do you want to bet that's the enemy stronghold?

I was glad to see that all my sneaking around was finally paying off.

"Sorry, kid—I won't be able to take you after all." The beast-man pressed his lighted staff into my hands and pointed to the bottom of the slope. "The village is straight down that path." Then he stabbed a finger at the smoke rising above the trees and added, "But don't go *that* way! Got it?!"

I'm supposed to be young, not brain dead.

"Pops!" I called to him as he bolted away.

The man kept running, but craned his head back. "What?"

"Er . . . what's your name?"

"Duclis!" he shouted. "We'll meet again!" Even as he spoke, his form vanished into the darkness.

For an enemy, Duclis seemed like an okay guy. I was glad I hadn't picked a fight with him, and not just because he probably would've wiped the floor with me.

It was time to get moving. I stowed Duclis' staff in the nearby brush and ran up the path as fast as I could.

***

After an awkward scramble in the darkness, I finally found what I was looking for: just above me on the hilltop stood an ancient, decrepit building. Like the old coliseum, its walls were crumbling, and sections of it had actually collapsed and left heaps of broken masonry on the hillside. The building had probably been abandoned by its original owners before Krotz and his cult had claimed it.

I'm pretty sure the land I stood on was once part of the Letidius Kingdom, which was wiped out five hundred years ago, but remnants of its civilization still dot the landscape in the form of crumbling ruins.

After scoping out all sides of the building, I discovered only one entrance. Luckily, it wasn't guarded. Magic lighting filtered dimly out of a gaping hole on one side of the building, which was most likely the place where all the commotion had come from. I figured it was best to stay away from that side.

The people occupying the building, I gathered, were probably all from the cult's upper echelon. Judging from the scant signs of activity, there weren't nearly enough of them for a building that huge.

Getting in didn't seem like it would pose a problem, but considering that my recent track record with risk assessment had been pretty lousy, I decided to play it safe. All I knew was that there was someone in that building capable of setting off an explosion—and a damn loud one at that. There was always the chance that it wasn't an enemy, that Xelloss was the one exploding the crap out of that place. Maybe he'd managed to pursue Mazenda all the way here and was duking it out with her? It was an encouraging thought—not likely, but encouraging.

Or maybe, I thought, *Gourry got discovered sneaking in, and now mages with explosions are trying to kill him.* That was a much less encouraging thought.

I knocked my palm against my head. I didn't have time to get carried away with what-ifs! If an enemy attacking either Xelloss or Gourry had caused that explosion, I wasn't about to just sit back and watch.

I leapt out of the thicket I'd been hiding in and sprinted toward the building's entrance. I quieted my footsteps as I closed in on the large, square hole that served as an open doorway. I didn't sense anyone in the immediate vicinity, which was a good sign.

The building's façade was lined with white pyroxene pillars, all of which were cracked and half covered by dirt and sand. I passed through the doorless opening and into a large rounded hall. Light filtered in from somewhere on the right. Guessing that was the place to head, I took a step forward.

KA-BOOM!

There are a lot of those today.

The explosion had gone off somewhere within the building— there was a battle in progress, no doubt about it. I braced myself and dashed toward the light. I quickly discovered that that section of the main hall split off into two passages: one corridor went straight for a bit and then turned, the other led to a stairway. The strange light filtered out from both passages.

"Crap!" I griped. All I had right then was intuition, and one false move could ruin everything. After an exasperating couple of seconds, I picked the winding corridor.

Peering around its bend, I saw that the passageway had doors lining each wall and went on for a ways before taking a sharp right. In spite of its age, the interiors of the building seemed really strong and preserved; the place had probably been a holiday party mansion of sorts for lesser nobility back in the day.

Before venturing farther down the corridor, I checked to see if I could sense anyone behind the doors. No one was there so I took the right and found yet another corridor lined with still more doors. *Great*, I thought sarcastically, then took off down the passage, running.

Luckily, that corridor ended far more promisingly—with a smoking chamber, its door blown apart by some sort of explosion spell. I smiled triumphantly as I carefully stepped over steaming hunks of door.

The room was empty. One of the chamber's walls, I noticed, had been spectacularly destroyed, and revealed the nighttime mountain scenery outside.

It was definitely the work of magic. In fact, it had probably been the wall blowing up during my run-in with Duclis—it explained the bleeding light I'd seen from outside the building.

I spun around and charged back down the corridor. I wanted to check out the rooms that I rushed past, but something drove me on, an immediate sense of urgency that I couldn't shake. All I knew was that I had to retrace my steps and find my way into the main hall again.

Unfortunately, I ran into someone at the bend in the corridor.

"Hey," snarled a familiar voice. "Where do you think you're going?"

I looked up into a memorably hideous face: Vedur. The great sword he held low in his right hand glistened.

Damn! my brain screamed.

Luckily, I still had my mask on, so Vedur didn't know who he was looking at. Realizing he could very well recognize my voice, I quickly reverted to my kiddie whine.

"A-after the meeting ended," I sniveled, "I got split off from Daddy." I fiddled with my thumbs and shuffled my feet. "I-I was wandering around when something went boom. I just came to find out what it was." I whimpered a little and rubbed my nose on my sleeve. I was beginning to think my act was working and that I'd be out of that jam soon enough when—

"Take your mask off," Vedur barked.

Again with the mask! *If the cult hates the things so damn much, you'd think they'd take them off the dress code.*

There were no reasonable options left. The time for drastic measures had arrived.

I quickly strategized. The corridor we stood in was fairly wide, but it wasn't wide enough for Vedur to take a good swing at me with that sword of his. I figured that if I could blind Vedur for a few seconds, that might give me the time I needed to slip past him and run for my life. If anyone else was in the building and heard the commotion, I had to hope I could scatter them while escaping.

"My mask?" I twittered, trying to stall the inevitable. "Oh, you mean *this* mask?"

I pressed my wrists together at my chest and began mumbling a spell under my breath. In case you're still wondering, it was Amplification.

"I said, take it *off*," Vedur growled as he took a menacing step closer. I pulled back and completed chanting the Amplification spell. I started to chant a fireball, but it needed just a few more—

"Take it off or I cut you up!" Vedur snapped as his hand tightened around the hilt of his sword. He was about to make a move when another familiar asshole interrupted him.

"Careful, Vedur!" came Gilfa's voice out of the darkness, seemingly from out of nowhere. "He's—"

Thanks to Gilfa unintentionally throwing Vedur off for a half second, I managed to finish my spell just as Vedur took the hint.

Too late, beast-man!

"Fireball!"

As a rule of thumb, don't use a fireball indoors—not if you value your furniture, anyway. But with my magic strength downgraded for the time being, I figured the spell would be effective enough without causing massive damage.

As the spell's power gathered, though, a strange sensation radiated from between my joined palms. My eyes widened. Something very destructive was about to happen, and I didn't have much time to react.

Uh oh.

"Vedur!" Gilfa's voice roared. "Pull back!"

As he spoke, a fiery ball of light formed between my hands. I flung it at Vedur with everything I had.

BOOOOOM!

The explosion knocked me backward and slammed my butt against the floor. The roar shuddered through the entire corridor. When I tentatively opened my eyes and looked up, I saw no sign of Vedur. He was either very dead or very lucky.

The floor and walls were scorched and cracked, and the corridor had collapsed and become completely impassable. The biggest question of the moment was: who or what had caused that explosion? Me? That didn't seem likely for a sealed sorceress.

Time for a test.

Hastily, I chanted another spell.

"Lighting!"

As I released the spell, a brightly shining globe glowed directly above my head. The lighting spell looked like it was functioning at full power, but I hadn't activated the amplification spell. That could only mean . . . !

"Hell, yeah!" I cried as I jumped to my feet and whipped off my mask. One way or another, Xelloss had come through for me.

Maybe it had been a bit rash of me to amplify the fireball's power before checking to see if my powers had come back. But let me say that amplification is the way to go if you want to wreak some serious havoc. I gazed at the smoking and destroyed corridor and, I have to admit, got incredibly stoked.

Bring it on!

Still, I was lucky that the spell's barrier had apparently gotten stronger as well. Without that, I would've been reduced to a heap of ash and teeth.

With the passageway plugged up, I figured the best way back into the main hall was to go through the blown wall in the innermost chamber and loop around outside. Of course, with my magic power restored and my talismans working nicely, I naturally wanted to try them both together again. I figured an amplified version of Dam Brass could smash a shortcut hole through the nearest wall *and* let me gauge how much more powerful the amplification made the spell. Like killing two birds with one stone! And to those of you who think I was just tripping on my new powers, the Dam Brass plan was in the interest of science.

I went into one of the rooms off the corridor and positioned myself facing the main hall. I chanted the amplification spell followed by Dam Brass.

BOOM!

With just a single shot, I blasted apart a hole in the wall large enough for an adult to walk through. The power in my fingertips was absolutely *dizzying*.

"Well, then," I chuckled to myself. "I'd best be outta here."

I approached the hole I'd just made, but then halted as I sensed something. I picked up a piece of rubble lying on the floor and casually tossed it outside. I'm grateful that what happened next happened to the rubble and not to me; out of a corner in the opening, just out of my sight, a silver light flashed. It sent the two halves of the now-bisected bit of rubble rolling across the floor.

"I guess you figured we'd be waiting for you, eh?" cackled Gilfa's disembodied voice. It came from the other side of the wall.

"Guess you two are sneakier than I thought," I drawled.

Vedur's head appeared in the hole. But, as usual, there was no sign of Gilfa; I guessed he was in the shadows again, so to speak.

"Where do we fight?" Vedur asked matter-of-factly, like he was asking where the bathroom was.

"Mmm." I considered for a moment. "Somewhere where I get a lot of breathing room so I don't have to smell you as much. Let's try the main hall."

The beast-man growled at my reply. Apparently he didn't like opponents with sass. He slid away quietly, and I jumped out through the hole in the wall and carefully followed.

That's right, I thought as I bore my gaze into his back. *No funny business, snake.*

I had to stay on my toes; powers restored or not, there were *two* jerks to deal with, and quite possibly a bunch more waiting elsewhere in the building. I knew I could blow Vedur and his shadowy friend to smithereens with my new amplification spell, but that would require a hell of a lot of chanting—more chanting than I could probably pull off in a tight battle. To top it all off, I still didn't have a handle on the severity of the amplified spells. If I used my powers haphazardly, I could bring the whole building down on my head.

I wanted plenty of room and sturdy walls that wouldn't collapse if I tried something big. The main hall fit both those requirements, a fact I confirmed once I stepped into it again with Vedur.

"Lighting!"

The shout came from Gilfa. Instantly, the spell created a light that hovered near the ceiling.

Vedur, not two dozen paces in, whipped around to me and assumed a fighter's crouch. "Let's go," he snarled, and before I could respond, he sprinted across the hall.

I took a surprised step back. *Easy!* I thought quickly. *Aren't we supposed to shake hands or something first?*

Rather than swinging his great sword, he rushed with its point forward and aimed for my chest. Dodging right or left would get me nailed with a slash for sure. I leapt backward while chanting a spell; at the same time, I heard Gilfa chanting something of his own.

"Elmekia Lance!" I shouted.

It was a great strategy on my part—the Elmekia Lance directly targets an opponent's mind, so Vedur's lesser-demon-level magic resistance wasn't going to help him. Unfortunately, none of that mattered, since he slid off to the side and evaded the damn thing.

At least his dodge veered him a bit off course and slowed him down momentarily. I took that blink-of-an-eye opportunity to pull farther back and begin chanting my next spell. Gilfa still finished first.

"Shadow Web!"

Vedur's shadow distorted and released spear-like tentacles straight for me. I leapt even farther back; the shadow spears shot across the room and stuck fast to the floor, dangerously close to my feet.

Vedur had, by then, recovered his balance, and he charged at me again with his sword. I prepared to dodge him, but then suddenly realized something very disheartening.

I couldn't move.

My eyes flew to my feet. The shadow spears had done their work: Gilfa's lances had plunged into my shadow on the floor, effectively pinning me to the spot where I stood. He'd done a Shadow Snap with the shadows under his control.

Bad! Very bad!

But I caught onto Gilfa's game too late; Vedur was already raising his great sword over his head. I crouched and threw my arms over my face, pathetically hoping that would do something as he brought his sword down.

SHINK!

A silver flash glinted through the air and deflected Vedur's blade. With a hard metallic sound, an unexpected sword clanged to the floor between the beast-man and me.

Someone had launched a sword at Vedur, repelling his blade within a hair's breadth of . . . well, my hair. I only knew one person with sword aim like that, and only one who would stupidly risk—and ultimately save—my life with such an insane move.

"Gourry!" I cried.

A familiar voice rang out from somewhere behind me, but it wasn't Gourry's.

"Your guess is a little off," my savior said coolly. "Try again."

I spun around with my eyes wide. "Zelgadiss?!"

3: NO REST FOR THE WEARY

"Lighting!" Zelgadiss boomed.

Under the blazing globe of light Zel created, my shadow disappeared. I took advantage of my newly freed movements and rushed over to join him.

Zelgadiss and I had been through some scrapes together. He was a chimera: part sorcerer, part rock golem, and part blow demon. To the best of my knowledge—and judging from the fact that his skin was still rocky—he hadn't finished his search for a way to regain his human form.

"Thanks," I panted as I reached him. "It's been awhile, Zel. What are you doing here?"

"I ought to be asking you the same thing," Zelgadiss replied, gesturing to my disguise and the amplification talismans. "What are you—um—wearing? And where's Gourry?"

I shook my head. "Long story," I muttered. "Let's talk about the details later."

"Right."

"My," giggled Gilfa's disembodied voice. "It's been awhile, Zelgadiss."

I blinked at Zelgadiss. "You know that guy?"

"Sort of," Zelgadiss murmured, keeping his eyes locked on Vedur.

"Coming after me all the way out here, in the middle of nowhere." Gilfa's voice cackled disdainfully. "So you're one of those 'Battle Between Light and Dark' types, hm? Let me give you some advice: your skin might be tough as rock, but one slice from Vedur's sword and you'll be nothing but rubble."

"Thanks," Zelgadiss snapped, "but I already knew that."

Zelgadiss, I noticed, was eyeing his sword across the hall. Since Vedur did the same, I figured my pal needed backup.

"Give me a sec," I whispered, then quickly chanted a spell. I threw up my arms.

"Lighting!"

I targeted the spell at Vedur's eyes. No matter how high his magic resistance, it didn't change the fact that bright light hurts your peepers.

Zelgadiss took off for his sword at a run. Vedur flinched and threw an arm over his face, but the light didn't stop him long. He squinted his eyes against my spell and charged right for Zelgadiss, closing the distance between the two of them before Zel could reach his sword.

"Zel!" I cried as Vedur swung with a roar.

"Lighting!"

This time, it was Zelgadiss casting the spell. He twisted himself away from Vedur and thrust his own light straight into the beast-man's exposed eyes.

"GAAAAH!" Vedur cried, staggering back.

With the light blinding him, Vedur swung his sword but hit nothing but floor. Zelgadiss rolled, recovered his sword, and jumped back to his feet. Without sparing another second, he dove sword-first for Vedur.

"Vedur!" Gilfa screamed. "Look—"

But it was too late. Zelgadiss thrust his sword hilt-deep into Vedur's throat, splattering blood in all directions.

The beast-man twitched and trembled, then slowly tilted forward. As he did, I noticed him raise his great sword again and hoist it high over his head so he could bring it down on Zelgadiss.

"Hey!" I cried, shocked that Vedur was still conscious enough to move.

Without any time to withdraw his sword, Zelgadiss leapt backward, his sword lodged in Vedur's throat.

Shakily, Vedur's fingers gripped the hilt of Zel's sword. He slowly extracted the blade from his neck, then let it fall to the floor with a clang. His body shook as he awkwardly backed away.

Unreal!

Zelgadiss and I stared at each other, awestruck. The blade had impaled Vedur right through the throat—that's one of the most fatal strikes you can launch, and even the biggest, baddest creatures in the world can't survive without a neck. But Vedur had just pulled the sword out and stalked away to shake it off, like he'd yanked a splinter from his foot. It was completely impossible! Was Vedur just spasming in his final death throes or something?

Still, there was something strange about the way Vedur moved. He strode forward in an unusually erratic fashion, like he was possessed by another power.

It was more than a little creepy. Zel and I watched Vedur disappear into the corridor.

"What the hell was that all about?" Zelgadiss mumbled slowly.

"Um, he's got more spunk than I thought?" I ventured. "But otherworldly spunk or not, I'm going after him. Enemies should have the decency to die when they're killed."

Zelgadiss looked at me like I was insane. "And just what are you planning to do?"

"Good question." I thought about that for a second. Vedur had vanished deeper into the building, so my hunch was that he'd gone off to . . .

"Follow him with me?" I asked. "My friend Amelia's been captured, so he may lead us straight to her."

Zelgadiss mulled that one over. "Was she the one who caused the explosion earlier? The one that blew a hole in the side of the building?"

"Probably." If indiscriminate blowing-up was the goal, Amelia was your girl.

I went over how things might've gone down. Assuming Xelloss was right and Mazenda had sealed Amelia's magic, Amelia—discovering that Mazenda's magic seal on her was finally broken—had probably destroyed the wall to try and escape but had then bumped into Krotz and his people. Being conveniently in the vicinity, Zelgadiss must've seen the explosion and come over to investigate. He'd probably arrived right after me.

"Fine." Zelgadiss nodded. "Let's go."

The two of us dashed off, hot-footing it after Vedur.

***

For someone supposed to be dead, Vedur could walk pretty fast. At least we found a very clear trail to follow—blood, buckets of it, spattering the floor and walls of the corridor—so seeing where he'd gone was easy enough.

The trail took us up the stairway to a narrow corridor that went deeper into the building. Vedur took a right at the entrance and turned his head to glance back at us.

He didn't look good, to say the least. I had no idea how he'd gone so long after losing all that blood. And speaking of blood, it seemed to have stopped gushing from the gash at his throat. Nothing about him seemed alive, yet there he was, his eyes glazed over and his mouth half open.

Chills ran up my spine when I looked into his inanimate eyes. Although his footing was all over the place and he didn't have the best coordination, he somehow still managed to lift his sword and angle it in our direction. I had the urge to ask him about Amelia's whereabouts, but who was I kidding? He wasn't up for conversation.

"You don't look too good, Vedur," Zelgadiss said flatly. He closed in on the snake man as he spoke, his own blade lowered. "Don't worry; you'll be out of your misery shortly."

As if in response to Zelgadiss' comment, a low voice began chanting a spell from somewhere I couldn't place. *Great*, I thought, *Gilfa again!*

Zelgadiss had picked up on Gilfa, too. "I don't think so!" he snapped as he sprinted for Vedur. Gilfa took the opportunity to spring one of his old tricks.

"Zel!" I cried. "Look out!"

The beast-man's shadow distorted, transforming into dozens of black blades that launched themselves at Zelgadiss. Zel leapt backward, ducking his head low and narrowly avoiding the lances.

"Damn!" he grunted as he retreated back to my side of the corridor. Zelgadiss' skin was like armor, and I sincerely doubted the blades could penetrate it, but there was no sense in testing that theory at the moment.

We had to get rid of Gilfa. Stupid, smarmy, wanting-a-fist-in-the-mouth Gilfa.

"So," I heard Zelgadiss murmur after a moment. "*That's* it."

I stared at him. *What's it?* Whatever it was, it made my somber rock buddy crack a dark little smile.

He turned to me. "Can your spells do something about that shadow?"

I frowned. "Well, Lighting can probably handle a simple Shadow Snap, but the Shadow Master spell's not that easy to deal with."

Zelgadiss paused. "Fine," he muttered, assuming an attack stance. "Then I'll just have to manage."

He suddenly broke into a charge toward Vedur, whose shadow, by the way, rose in preparation for another attack. This time it morphed into an inky black net that quickly spread across Zel's path.

Zelgadiss growled. But rather than halt in his tracks (as I half expected him to do), he just launched himself forward with even more fervor. The net suddenly transformed into a black, mountain-like shape barbed with long, tapered needles

No, no, no—don't hit that!

Zelgadiss was charging too fast to even *think* about putting on the brakes. I froze, sure he was a goner . . . until a voice suddenly rang out.

"Flow Break!"

I whipped around. "Amelia!"

Light flooded the corridor, blinking out the shadow under Gilfa's control. Sensing his opportunity, Zelgadiss lunged.

Vedur hoisted his sword up to meet him. He and Zelgadiss slammed hard into each other then went crashing to the floor. After a few seconds, only one of them got up again: Zelgadiss.

"That was close," he panted, breathing hard. He turned to the figure clad in white, standing deeper in the corridor. "Thank you."

I waved to her. "Amelia!" I called. "Long time no see!"

Amelia bounded over, an adrenaline smile plastered across her face. "Glad you made it here, Miss Lina!" she chirped. "How are things with you?"

"Pretty good. Oh, this is Zelgadiss. He's a friend."

I paused. *Daaaa! What the hell am I doing?!*

I stopped my blathering. There was no time for small talk considering the danger we were in.

With a wary stance, I threw my gaze around the room. "Gilfa's gotta be around here somewhere," I said quickly. "Zel, did you see him?"

Zelgadiss shook his head. "He's already dead."

"Yeah, so we'd better—huh?" I turned to him. "What do you mean he's dead?"

"Take a look." Zelgadiss turned Vedur's body over with his foot and gave it a little kick for good measure. Then he reached down and slowly withdrew his sword from where he'd lodged it—in the hump on Vedur's back.

"He was hiding in there," Zelgadiss said as he pointed to the slashed and bloodied hump.

"Wha—?" Either Zelgadiss was nuts, or I was in for a hell of an explanation.

I kneeled down. On closer inspection, it looked like Vedur was an artificially created being, probably developed by Krotz himself. And Krotz, it looked like, had grafted a *second brain* onto the beast-man's back. Though Vedur's own brain had clearly been in command of his body at first, Gilfa's brain had probably taken over motor control after Vedur's mortal stabbing. It certainly explained the postmortem jerky walk.

To my disgust, I also noticed a small but visible seam that crossed the hump's wrinkly surface. *Gilfa's mouth,* I thought, which explained why we'd never located the origin of his voice. I guessed that Gilfa probably had "eyes" somewhere, too, but I didn't want to go snooping around for those. "If Krotz created this . . . thing," I finally muttered, choking down my nausea, "he is one real sicko."

"Miss Lina," Amelia chimed in, "we don't have time for this right now. The enemy could be here any second!"

"Enemy? How many enemies, roughly?"

"I'm not sure." Worry dampened the usual cheeriness in her voice. "I was running too fast from them to get a good look." She took a deep breath, then added, "But there's one we really have to watch out for."

"Who?" I asked, but regretted it immediately. I probably didn't want to know.

"Well . . ." Amelia squinted in puzzlement. "It's hard to say. While I was spying on the cult members, I heard one of them say, 'More intruders have arrived!' and then another say, 'Let's use the weapon of last resort! Let's unleash *him!*' "

"'Unleash'?" Anything on a leash could only be bad, bad news.

"Hold on," Zelgadiss interjected. His rocky face went even ashier with dread. "They said they'd unleash *him?*"

"Um, yeah."

Zelgadiss exhaled a long, labored breath, then glared at Amelia and me.

"Run."

"Huh?" I replied.

"Run!" Zelgadiss repeated. "And hurry up about it!"

As he spoke, he gripped his sword and broke into a sprint back toward the stairway.

"Hey!" I shouted. "Not so fast!"

"We should run, too," Amelia noted. "I feel that might be for the best."

Amelia took off at Zelgadiss' heels. Since Zelgadiss knew the extent of my powers and Amelia was usually on when it came to sensing danger—*and* since neither of them had bothered waiting for my opinion on the matter—I figured, yeah, sure, retreating was the way to go.

"Hey!" I yelled as I hurried to follow. "Wait for me!"

The three of us fled the building and ran into the darkness of the surrounding woods. By the time we'd reached the trees, we were out of breath and delirious from panic; at least, Zelgadiss and Amelia were. I was just out of breath, since

I didn't know enough about whatever was after us to start panicking just yet.

"You know," I panted, slumping against a tree, "I could let loose a Dragon Slave or something and blow that mansion to kingdom come."

"We should just get out of here," Zelgadiss insisted. "Without our star player, we can't do anything!"

Star player? *Maybe the lack of oxygen's turning Zelgadiss nutty.*

He didn't explain himself, so I just rolled my eyes and dropped the subject.

***

We didn't rest long. A minute or two later we continued speeding down the mountain path, tripping and stumbling in the waning light of the moon. It was dangerous, obviously, like any situation where you could both fall and crack your skull *and* run into some horrible rampaging Monster of Death, so I decided to help our feet along: I chanted an amplified Ray Wing.

Ray Wing is a spell for high-speed flight, where the rate of travel and weight of passage are directly proportional to the ability of the spell-caster. Without amplification, hauling two additional people keeps Ray Wing from reaching a normal running speed, so the amplification was what saved the day. Er, night.

I grabbed onto Amelia and Zel. "Ray Wing!"

We lifted into the air. Just then, something shot out from behind us.

FWOOSH!

A silver light incinerated the ground directly below. The Ray Wing had barely saved us from becoming charcoal.

"What the hell?!" I cried. Amelia gripped me tightly, suddenly freaked, and Zelgadiss cursed creatively.

It had almost looked like . . . a Dragon Lord's Laser Breath. I certainly hoped I was seeing things.

In the darkness, I couldn't clearly make out where the beam had come from, but I could see the swath of trees ripped apart in its wake. The best I could tell, the light had originated from the direction of the cult's stronghold. I whipped my head around.

The area around the building's entrance was lit by a dull patch of moonlight. There, standing alone, a single figure watched us.

"Yikes," I muttered, trying to keep the panic from my voice. "I think that's our cue to go." With that, I raised our flight speed and got us out of there in a hurry.

***

"So what happened to you, Amelia? You never explained that part."

Amelia, Zelgadiss, and I had returned to Mane Village. We'd arrived at the hay barn on the outskirts of town where I'd stowed my things before venturing up into the mountains. The three of us had a lot of catching up to do.

"Well, nothing interesting," Amelia replied, shrugging her shoulders. "After the enemy captured me, that Mazenda woman sealed my magic and they locked me up in a room. Every once in a while, I'd test out my magic powers to see if they were, well, *unsealed*, but for the longest time they never were. Then all of a sudden they *were*, you know, unsealed, so I blew a hole in the wall. But before I could make a break for it, I bumped into a bunch of those guys, so . . ." Amelia trailed off into silence.

"So you fought your way back into the building and hid inside?"

"Right."

"Wait a second," Zelgadiss interjected. He was getting worked up again, like when he'd insisted we run like headless chickens. "Are you saying the enemy has someone with the power to seal spells?!"

"Easy," I said soothingly, hoping to calm Zelgadiss down. "I'm not entirely sure about that."

"You're not *sure?*"

"Well, after Amelia got captured, a priest named Xelloss showed up—"

"Xelloss?!" Zelgadiss shrieked, jumping up. I half expected his head to explode. "Xelloss is here?! *Here?!*"

"You know him?"

"All right, that's enough!" Amelia strode up and wedged herself between us. "We're stepping on each other's toes here. I think what we need to do is get the straight story from . . . er . . . Mister Zedilgass."

Zelgadiss rolled his eyes and sighed. "It's Zelgadiss," he and I said in unison.

The guy was pretty exhausted, and I couldn't blame him. He'd been on a grueling journey to try and find a way to get back his original human form after a certain nasty Red Priest—you probably know whom I'm talking about—turned Zel into a human-golem-blow-demon chimera. And according to the brief update Zelgadiss had given me on our flight into Mane, he wasn't much closer to reaching his goal.

He slowly sat down on a bale of hay and lowered his face into his hands. After a minute, he glanced up at Amelia.

"You've heard about my quest, right?"

She nodded. "You want your human body back."

"Right. I'm still not even sure that's possible, but I've tried talking to countless apothecaries, sorcerers, and alchemists all over the place. The closest thing I ever got to an answer came from a chimerical researcher I once met in a tavern.

"I was trying to, well . . ." He trailed off for a second. "I was trying to *soften* my troubles with some wine when he dumped his juice into my cup. He showed me how easy it was to mix the two, but then he asked me to try and separate the drinks again." He sighed. "He told me it was theoretically possible, but not easy. I appreciated the metaphor and all, but he still ruined my drink and spilled half his juice in my lap—I'm pretty sure it was the first nonalcoholic substance he'd had all day.

"Anyway, he told me that each life form has certain characteristics unique to itself. Birds, for instance, are born with wings and beaks, a specific body temperature, that sort of thing. Chimera manufacturing is a process that involves identifying common characteristics between two or more life forms and then melding them together using an intermediary.

"But with all the research going on, they're still having trouble finding technology that can separate a hybrid form into its individual parts again. He said it could take centuries to discover it—and that's assuming they can discover it at all." He rubbed his temples and sighed. "Needless to say, it was really bad news at the time. After waking up in the gutter the next morning, I went off in search of a more sober information source and heard a rumor about the Claire Bible."

I perked up at that. "The Claire Bible?"

"Well, a certain part of it, anyway. I heard it contained information on manufacturing a completely different sort of chimera, so I tracked down the family that owned it." His eyes darkened. "That's when I met Xelloss. I found out he was after the manuscript, too, as was Krotz and his cult. Krotz, obviously, got to the manuscript before us, killed the guy who owned it, and disappeared." Zelgadiss shook his head. "Now I have to beat the cult *and* Xelloss to get my hands on the thing."

"Beat Xelloss?" I repeated. "Were you planning to do that before hell froze over, or after?"

"That's not funny." He glared at me. "Xelloss and I formed a temporary alliance because of the whole Krotz thing. Technically he's my ally right now, but only until we beat the cult." Zelgadiss' tone was unwavering, almost businesslike. "I'll figure out what to do about Xelloss later."

I didn't want to burst his bubble, but it had to be said. "Zel," I said carefully, "even if you get your hands on the manuscript, there's no guarantee it'll solve your problems."

"I know that. I have no idea if the contents will tell me how to make myself human again, but that's a risk—"

"No," I cut in. Obviously, he wasn't catching my drift. "What I mean is that even if you or Xelloss manage to snag the manuscript, we have no confirmation that it's the real deal.

There are so many fraudulent manuscripts floating around; it could easily be one of those."

Zelgadiss blinked at me. "You mean Xelloss didn't tell you?"

Here we go again. More surprises!

"The caretaker of that manuscript was a direct descendant of the high priest who served in the court of Letidius." He rolled his eyes. "Xelloss is such a bastard."

Letidius, if you recall, was the king who ruled over that area some five centuries ago. He destroyed himself and his kingdom in his zealous quest for immortality, but legend has it that he gathered together a vast library full of knowledge pertaining to sorcery during his rule. Supposedly the collection was destroyed and its contents lost. I'd *thought* that the location of the lost Letidius capital was a little farther north.

"Supposedly," Zelgadiss explained, "this ancestor had the manuscript with him when he fled the dying kingdom."

If what Zelgadiss said was true, there was reason to believe the manuscript stolen by Krotz was indeed real. But there was still that margin of error.

"There's a fair chance," I countered, "that the manuscript was stolen or corrupted over time. The family might've *thought* they had the authentic manuscript when, in fact, it was plundered, right under their noses, generations ago and replaced with a fake."

Zelgadiss, however, wasn't fazed by my comments. "One hundred and twenty years ago, the caretaker had the same doubts. Verification was simple: he did as the manuscript said and then observed the results." He stared meaningfully at me. "The result was a complete success. But, for reasons unknown, the chimera he created began to run amok. I'm sure you heard about the thing—Zanaffar, the Demon Beast of Sairaag?"

I froze. *Zanaffar?!* I thought in shock. The legendary creature responsible for the destruction of Sairaag City? He'd just been a magic experiment gone wrong?!

As far as I knew, no record of explaining who the Demon Beast really was ever existed. Of course, it would come as no surprise if the original keepers of the manuscript had destroyed the proof to keep blame away from them. You'd have to be nuts to admit that it was you or one of your ancestors who accidentally destroyed the hometown of the Sorcerers' Guild.

"Is that stuff really true?" Amelia asked in a faint voice.

Zelgadiss shrugged his shoulders.

"If the owner wasn't bluffing," I said, reasoning it all out, "and creating such a creature is actually possible, then Krotz and his cult . . ." It was too stomach-churning a thought to say out loud.

"They've already completed it." Zelgadiss took the liberty. "Zanaffar Number Two."

My stomach . . . well, churned.

"I didn't think they'd complete the task so quickly," he added, "but there you have it."

"So the 'star player' you referred to earlier is Gourry, right?" I asked.

"Yeah. If the legends are true, then only the warrior of the Sword of Light can defeat Zanaffar." Zelgadiss crossed his arms and frowned. "But he's not around, is he?"

"It's too early to give up!" Amelia suddenly exclaimed, rising from her bale of hay. Half a second later, she successfully surprised no one by starting up her fist-clenching and shouting routine.

"Even without Mister Gourry," she declared, "if we combine our strength, then—"

"Get over it!" I interrupted. "You really think we've got a shot? Get serious!"

Sorry, but I'm really not in the mood.

That sure shut her up. A cold look channeled into her eyes and she sat back down on the hay.

"Not really," she muttered gloomily, fiddling with a piece of straw.

The truth was out and even Amelia had to admit it. She looked up at me, her forehead wrinkled, and asked, "Exactly how powerful is this chimera going to be?"

I let out a breath and thought for a moment. "There are a few things we can guess," I replied at last. "We know that his predecessor was the one who destroyed Sairaag, right? So it's safe to assume that the new Zanaffar will have an insane amount of offensive power, too. If he's allowed to attack, he could destroy an entire city. We have to try and keep him from doing that." I bowed my head and scowled, trying to think of some method for fighting a creature like that.

"First of all, if this chimera's really that powerful, there's no way the Sword of Light could wound him, regardless of the legend. The Sword is definitely powerful, but it's still an imprecise weapon; the wielder would never even get close enough to take a swing at the damn thing.

"Second," I continued, "this isn't the same Zanaffar. It's a new one, maybe a better one. And there's a real possibility that this new one will go berserk like the first Zanaffar did." I smacked my palm on a nearby pile of hay. "If they make a dozen or two dozen Zanaffars to see if the magic in the manuscript is for real, then we've got one ugly situation on our hands. It could make the attack on Sairaag look like a picnic.

"Third . . ." I paused, not wanting to say it. "Third, it's clear that offensive spells have no effect on Zanaffar.

"Let's not forget, Sairaag was the City of Sorcery. There were probably plenty of sorcerers capable of using Dragon

Slave–level spells against Zanaffar, but since the Demon Beast still managed to raze the city, we can only conclude that Zanaffar had nearly flawless magic resistance."

Amelia's jaw dropped. "What do you *mean* magic won't work?!"

"To find the answer to that, you must first ponder the true nature of magic."

Look who's back.

Zelgadiss' face twitched with displeasure as Amelia turned toward the new speaker in surprise. I didn't even bother glancing at the door.

"How long have you been standing there, Xelloss?" I asked tiredly.

"Ever since the young lady's line about using the power of conviction to defeat the Demon Beast." Xelloss entered the barn, his staff making small taps on the ground as he walked, and crouched casually beside me on the straw-covered floor. He smiled at Amelia. Unused to the man, she cringed uncomfortably.

"Don't worry, Amelia," I said with a dismissive wave of my hand. "He's not an enemy—not right now, anyway."

"A rather accurate assessment," Xelloss agreed.

I nodded my head at him. "I owe you one, Xelloss. Thanks for getting me my spells back."

145

He shrugged. "You're welcome."

I paused. "So what happened to Mazenda?" I asked carefully. I wondered if he could sense how anxious I was to hear the answer to that one.

But Xelloss didn't miss a beat. "She was destroyed," he responded simply, that steady, somewhat absent-minded smile never leaving his face.

Amelia gasped. "How?!"

Xelloss touched his forefinger to his lips. "It's a secret."

Amelia screwed up her face. *Welcome to our world*, I wanted to tell her.

"H-how'd you even know we were here?"

"Ah." Xelloss' tone remained calm, almost sagelike, as if he could anticipate any question and serve up the correct answer piping hot. "I simply traced the magic energy given off by the talismans I sold Miss Lina."

I'd forgotten about that. Using sorcery to scry for a specific kind of magic energy is a common strategy among sorcerers, but it's only useful if the one doing the scrying knows the magic's specific energy pattern. My talismans were basically tracking devices for Xelloss; I told myself to remember that.

"So," Xelloss went on, joining his palms as he organized his thoughts, "back to the 'why-won't-magic-work' question. In the first place, magic—" He broke off there and paused. "Rather, let's backtrack a bit. What is mana?"

"A force that originated before the creation of this world," Amelia recited as though she'd memorized the response long ago.

"Precisely. Because magic originates from a place of nothingness, it is capable of altering the fate of this world either through producing power or through other means."

I took a seat next to Amelia, and Zelgadiss leaned against a stack of hay. We weren't about to ignore the man.

"When we invoke magic here in the physical world, the spell acts as a medium to draw power from the astral side. Think of the astral side as the backside of the world; the boundary separating it and us is paper-thin.

"Elemental spells—earth, water, fire, and air—are manifestations of physical forces. These spells may be extremely powerful, but because they are embodiments of physical concepts, physical defenses can protect against them.

"However," Xelloss raised his forefinger again to make his point, "mind-affecting sorcery and half of the offensive spells in Black Magic attack the opponent's astral self directly from the astral side."

"Teacher," I piped in, raising a hand only half-jokingly. "I have a question."

"Yes?"

"Gaav Flare has a visible trail of flame, and Dragon Slave can directly destroy a castle or even a mountain. The last time I checked, mountains and castles weren't astral phenomena."

Yeah, I can be a little snotty, but that's how I keep people on their toes.

"Mmm," Xelloss hummed. "I'm glad you brought that up. With the Dragon Slave, you can see a faint red beam as the spell makes for and converges with its target. Gaav Flare's flames and Dragon Slave's red beam can all be thought of as the spells' fuses, so to speak."

"Fuses?"

"Indeed. The resulting reaction causes attack power from the astral side to converge at the target and manifest itself in this world. If the target is not alive, the power simply comes through, but if the target *does* live, its mental component is torn asunder and any remaining energy breaks through into our world.

"Of course," Xelloss added, "there are also spells like Elmekia Lance that solely affect the astral, but I'm sure you've noticed that difference before."

Damn! The guy was smart—nerd smart. I wished I had some way to jot all that information down.

If Gourry were here, I'm sure he'd be snoring in back of the barn by now.

"Another question?" It was Amelia asking this time.

"Yes?"

"Where'd you learn all this? Even the Sorcerers' Guild doesn't know that much about the true nature of sorcery."

Xelloss smiled. He arched his eyebrows and touched his lips.

"Let me guess," I muttered.

"The only answer I can give," he said, "is that the prevailing opinions of the Sorcerers' Guild are not the most refined theories on sorcery."

"I have a question," Zelgadiss snapped.

"You? Oh, anything."

"Are you going to get to the point some time today?"

Xelloss smiled. "Ah. Well, the reason offensive magic can't affect Zanaffar is because Zanaffar's mind is completely sealed off from the astral side."

My eyebrows furrowed. Sealed off?

"Zanaffar has a kind of wall between his physical side and his astral side. For that reason, the offensive astral power of Black Magic will never actually penetrate Zanaffar's mind or body. Such spells cannot damage him."

The barn grew quiet. It was extremely bad news for all of us.

Xelloss was quick to add, "The silver lining here is that the full offensive and physical power of Shamanic Magic can be utilized."

Amelia sucked in a breath happily.

"On the other hand," Xelloss admitted, "Zanaffar's hide is at least as resilient as an Arc Dragon's, possibly as tough as a Dimos Dragon's or a Dragon Lord's. His hide alone can easily deflect human-level Shamanic Magic."

Amelia released that breath, sad.

I didn't know if what Xelloss said was based on fact or was simply hypothesis, but it certainly made sense.

"So it's true," I said at last. "Zanaffar can only *really* be challenged by the Sword of Light or something like it."

"It also means we can't even hope to counterattack so long as we don't have Gourry." Zelgadiss sounded cranky and tired, like he'd lost the battle before it had even begun.

"Gourry?" Xelloss asked.

"He's got the Sword of Light."

For the first time since his arrival, Xelloss actually looked surprised at something. "Surely you're joking."

"The hell I am," I snapped. "I wouldn't be putzing around in the dark, hiding out in reeking barns and waiting around like a jackass for any other reason." I sighed with resignation.

It occurred to me that if I knew the Sword of Light's magical energy pattern, I could scry for it from the astral side. But I didn't know it, so I couldn't, and that left me back at square one.

Don't get me wrong. It wasn't like I hadn't *tried* to do research on the Sword. But every time I'd ask Gourry to lend it to me for even a minute, he'd look at me like I was insane. "What?" he'd say to me. "So you can run off with it?"

Do I look like the type of girl who'd try to run off with something like that?

Don't answer that.

Xelloss, meanwhile, was in his own little world. He seemed to be working something out in his head, and kept vocalizing little bits of what he was thinking.

"You mean he . . . um, wait . . . no, wait . . . that would mean . . ." He went on and on like that for a while, until he finally seemed to come to a conclusion. Taking a deep breath, he looked up at the three of us.

"Be that as it may, I'm afraid I can't spare any more time here. I only came by to observe your progress; I must be off."

He'd just turned to leave when Amelia grabbed hold of his robe and halted him mid-step. He paused.

"Um," he intoned, "would you mind letting go of my robe?"

"I don't think so." Amelia shook her head resolutely. "I don't know who you are, but there's an evil Demon Beast out there! If you make a wrong move, not only are *you* done for, but you'll put *our* mission in great jeopardy. My intuition tells me loud and clear not to let you go. Not by yourself."

Xelloss turned toward me. I couldn't tell if he was puzzled or ticked off; probably both.

"Can't you," he asked, "*do* something about her?" He pointed to Amelia like she was a dog that had peed on his shoe.

"Sorry," I said, baring my teeth in a mock-smile. "Can't do a thing. She's like that, totally hell-bent on risking her life for Truth, Love, and Justice."

Amelia, all fired up now, nodded resolutely at Xelloss.

"A strange one," Xelloss remarked.

"Yup."

Xelloss sighed. "I see," he murmured. "Quite a gay and merry bunch we have here, it would seem."

I scoffed and pointed a finger right back him. "You're the only one who's gay."

"N-not at all!" Xelloss stammered. "I'm perfectly straight! Perfectly straight!"

His protests weren't convincing, to say the least.

Zelgadiss had had enough of our shenanigans. He turned away, and I got the feeling that he thought we were a squabbling bunch of cretins. He had this I'm-gonna-keep-my-distance-from-these-cretins sort of look about him.

"A-anyway, I've had enough," Xelloss blustered. "I'm leaving!" With that, he stomped out of the barn.

Amelia squeaked.

"Amelia!" I snapped, furrowing my eyebrows disapprovingly. "Why'd you let him go?"

Amelia looked at her hand, its fingers still in a clasping position, then looked at me with wide eyes. "But I didn't! I swear!"

"Look, we can't just let him leave." I rushed out of the barn after Xelloss. "Xelloss, wait up!"

Outside, the morning sun had brightened the sky and warmed the air. To the east spanned the mountains, their peaks crowned with snow. They glowed peach and pink against the bright blue sky.

Since Xelloss didn't seem to want to talk to us, we just trailed him for a while. After a good half hour, he finally spun around on his heels and sighed disapprovingly.

"All right," he murmured. "Why are you all following me?"

"The more the merrier," I replied, flashing him a smile. "Two's better than one and four's better than two, don't you think? You can't deny that there's strength in numbers."

"No, I can't." He pursed his lips in resignation. "All right, have it your way. I shall go forward as I please, and you're free to follow as you please. Is that acceptable?"

I nodded eagerly. "Sure!"

Before you point it out, I was quite aware that I was making decisions without letting Amelia and Zelgadiss contribute, but I figured I was doing what was best for the group. Still, I had to get something out of the way before we finalized our four-person party.

"If your plan was to go off on your own," I asked Xelloss, "then why did you bother coming all this way only to look in on us?"

Xelloss waved a hand. "Because," he said simply, "didn't I promise you we'd reconvene in this village?"

The moment he finished his sentence, we all heard a KA-BOOM.

Our heads jerked in the direction of the sound. Partway up the mountain, where we knew the cult's stronghold stood, a thick cloud of dust hovered menacingly in the sky.

"I assume that's bad," Xelloss commented vaguely.

After the initial surprise, we hurried up the mountain path to get a closer look at what had happened. The cult's abandoned mansion hideout had been turned into an enormous crater, a wasteland of smoke and rubble. From the looks of it, the explosion had been caused by a Dragon Slave or something similar.

"W-who did this?" I wondered aloud.

"Evil shall always be destroyed!" Amelia proclaimed.

Just more nonsense. Ignore her.

Xelloss shrugged. "Master Krotz and his people, I suspect."

I whipped around to face him. *"Them?"* I asked incredulously. "But why?"

"Probably to avoid complaints. They can claim their headquarters was hit with a Dragon Slave and thus save face rather than admit your infiltration occurred because of poor security."

"Wait a minute," Zelgadiss interjected suspiciously. "How did you know *we* attacked this place last night?"

"Simple." He counted off on his fingers. "One: Miss Lina informed me earlier that Miss Amelia had been captured by the enemy. Two: you've been discussing Zanaffar. And three: as I entered the village last night, I noticed a flash go off in the mountains at precisely this location."

Zelgadiss thought for a minute. "I still don't see why they'd destroy their own headquarters and move on," he muttered. "With Zanaffar here, couldn't they just use him to fight us if we returned to attack?"

That sparked something in my brain. "Amelia," I said abruptly. "You said you heard them call Zanaffar a last resort, right? And if he was the one who shot that giant beam at us as we flew away from the headquarters, he never even tried to pursue. Krotz hasn't had the manuscript very long; maybe that means . . ."

"Ah!" Amelia slapped a fist against her palm. "Zanaffar probably isn't complete yet!" Her eyes were alight with the fire of conviction.

"Let's follow them!" she cried. "While Zanaffar, Demon Beast of the darkness, is not yet complete, we can use our power to smash the cult's evil ambitions!"

"I don't mind the smashing part," Zelgadiss remarked, "but do you have any idea where they ran off to, Justice Girl?"

Amelia was visibly deflated by the insult. "Uh . . ." Unable to come up with anything, she shot Xelloss a desperate look. "Don't *you* know? You must know!" She gripped his sleeve. "TELL ME!"

"I do *not*," Xelloss replied shortly. "All I can say is if Zanaffar truly is incomplete, then I imagine they're moving their base to another location as we speak." He paused. "In retrospect," he said more quietly, "I should have asked Mazenda about the cult's backup hideouts before I finished her off."

As our plans hit more and more dead ends, I realized that I hadn't shared a vital piece of information. I took a deep breath.

"I'm not sure where the hideout is," I said at last, tentatively pointing eastward, "but I think they're headed *that* way."

"What makes you say that?" Zelgadiss asked.

Before answering, I looked over at Amelia. It didn't seem like a good time to spring such crappy news on her, but I doubted a better one would come along.

Here goes nothing . . .

"Last night," I began, "I sneaked into the coliseum again. Krotz was giving a speech about the cult's future plans, and . . . well . . ." I struggled for a softer, easier way to put it, but there really wasn't one.

"They're gonna destroy Saillune."

"Whaaaaaaat?!"

Amelia reacted pretty much as I'd expected.

"W-why would they destroy Saillune?!" she cried. "How could they do such a thing?! And if Zanaffar's complete, they'll be able to do it!"

After about five seconds of panic, she set her jaw and stamped her foot. "We can't allow this!" she proclaimed. "We have to follow them. There's not a moment to lose!"

With that, she spun around and marched purposefully back toward the village. The rest of us scrambled to follow—at least, until she suddenly stopped dead in her tracks.

"Amelia?" I asked. I ran up and looked over her shoulder, then froze.

Before us, blocking our path, stood a small army of villagers. I could hear their hateful grumbling and see the sneers on their faces; they were out for blood, no doubt about it.

Xelloss caught up to us and looked out at the arrayed ranks. "Ah," he said, as nonchalantly as ever. "These must be Master Krotz's followers here to kill us."

"You!" a grizzled, middle-aged farmer yelled. He was obviously itching for a fight, and he didn't look like he would take no for an answer. "What the hell did you do with Master Krotz?!"

"It's them!" another man's voice rose up. "They're the ones who crashed the meeting the other day!"

The bloodlust I sensed from the group was off the charts. If I'd been alone with my powers still sealed, I would've been as good as dead.

My mind returned to the newly destroyed stronghold. *Of course!* I thought. By blowing up his own headquarters in such a spectacular way, Krotz had not only annihilated all evidence that he was "building" Zanaffar, but he'd incited his followers to rise against us. A hundred ordinary villagers were no match for us, but the mob still acted as a barricade; it would slow our progress, buying Krotz time as he went about putting the pieces of his plan into place.

That magnificent bastard—I couldn't *wait* to kill him!

"I suppose we have no choice," Xelloss commented casually. "We must dispose of them in one blow." He began to walk forward.

Uh oh.

"H-hold on!" I called. "Wait a sec, Xelloss!"

Xelloss stopped in mid-step and glanced back, perplexed.

"What's wrong?" he asked. "Surely you're not going to try and sell me on their good points."

"No one in the world would mistake *them* for saints," I agreed. "But what good will it do if you kill the lot of them? Don't you realize the village needs these men? If you wipe them out, you'll be wiping out Mane!"

"I am aware," Xelloss answered simply.

For a second, I was stumped. I had no idea how to reason with the guy; he was dead-set on a massacre that morning.

"If you do," I told him, "you'll make mass murderers of us all. These are ordinary villagers who haven't committed any crimes." I stepped in between him and the crowd and, staring dead into his eyes, shook my head. "I can't let you do it."

As I spoke, I felt the villagers' bloodlust levels surge even higher behind me. They hadn't yet worked up the guts to attack us, but, as their rage grew by the second, I knew it was just a matter of time before something really nasty happened.

"All we need is to create a break through their center line," I argued, trying to offer a more humane solution. "Something that'll scatter them and give us room to hurry through."

Xelloss closed his eyes for a moment. "All right," he said at last. "I shall proceed with due gentleness." He then walked calmly toward the mob and began chanting a spell.

"Hey!" one of the men cried out. "What's that one doing?!"

Xelloss slowly arced his right hand through the air. He finished his chanting, then spoke the Power Words. I couldn't hear what he said, but it was impossible not to notice what happened next.

FWOOOSH!

A gust of wind swelled up out of nowhere and ripped through the crowd, parting it and forming a wide pathway for us. Under the violent whoosh of the wind, we heard the screams of the villagers as they were tossed aside like toys.

I gathered that Xelloss' spell had been a Diem Wing bumped up in power level—several times over, by the looks of it.

The villagers that had called for our deaths mere moments before now lay scattered and moaning. Some were caught high up in the trees; others lay tangled up in bushes or passed out in the dirt.

"Now," Xelloss announced, "let's be off." He started down the path, stopping briefly to address a few villagers who'd rolled back into the way.

"Would you mind moving?" he asked. "I'd rather not have to clear the path again."

The stragglers let out small screams and scurried into the bushes on either side of the mountain path.

So that was due gentleness.

***

Our progress sucked. Four days out of Mane, we still hadn't caught up with Krotz and his gang nor did we have any idea how far ahead they might be. Since we didn't have the slightest clue as to where their new hideout was, the best we could do was stop at a new village each day and keep our ears to the ground for any rumors. What nagged at me constantly—not unlike the rocks that kept shimmying their way into my boots—was the worry that we'd already passed Krotz's hideout without realizing it.

We also couldn't find out how close Krotz was to completing Zanaffar. A quick experiment proved that the Demon Beast's mind was protected against astral-side scrying, so that didn't help us. For all we knew, Zanaffar was done and ready to wreak havoc; it was a less than heartening thought.

There was something I did, though, that I knew *would* help: spell research. I couldn't very well go into battle without fully understanding how the talismans amplified my powers, but even more important, I wanted to look into a group of spells that I liked to call, "Spells that Should Work but Don't."

You see, some spells in the world of sorcery don't activate from the mere act of chanting them, even if you pull off the chant perfectly. For those spells, you have to go further and determine each one's specific parameters—some need special tools, some need ceremonies, and some have to be cast at very particular times. It's possible that all that special pain-in-the-neck detail is simply because the caster needs extra magic capacity; Xelloss' Blast Bomb, an obvious doozy, is just such a spell.

And yes, I had my own stock of "special need" spells. And yes, since I was in a position to amplify the hell out of my magic, I felt the need to experiment with those spells. So, while we kept on in our pursuit of Krotz and his gang, I spent every extra minute I could spare on spell research.

It was in the interest of science, I tell you. Science!

***

Amelia badgered me about my research every morning as we left our village-of-the-day. The fourth day out of Mane was no exception to that rule.

"I bet I can guess the spell you tried last night," Amelia muttered as we walked.

"Oh yeah?" was my response. That, and sticking my tongue out at her.

"Don't get cute," Zelgadiss snapped. His tone was cross, but his expression was more tired than angry. "The next time you 'experiment' in the middle of the night, pick a forest farther away from our inn."

Xelloss chimed in with that same indecipherable smile on his face. "That was quite the light show you put on last night," he commented. "You had the whole village in an uproar, Miss Lina. What exactly were you practicing?"

"Oh," I said with a wave of my hand, trying to downplay everyone's alarm. "A little of this, a little of that. But an amplified Dragon Slave sure makes a lot of noise, huh? Who'd'a thunk?"

I admit I should've known better, but seriously, I hadn't thought I'd take down the whole forest in a blazing inferno. You live, you learn.

"Hey," I added, assuming a more serious tone, "notching up my spell power a little each day and testing it out means my magic's gonna deliver when it counts. When I consider the future benefits of my experiments, I can overlook a little wide-scale destruction, can't you?"

The group walked on in dead silence.

Guess not.

"We don't want to impede your research," Xelloss said at last, "but if you drop the ball 'when it counts,' Master Krotz and his followers aren't going to be as forgiving as those villagers."

And with that, Xelloss halted. The rest of us followed suit a half second later. We all stared into the thicket beside the path.

"You can quit hiding in the bushes," I called out. "We know you're in there."

Something snorted. "Not bad," it muttered. "Nothing gets past you."

A moment later, the bushes stirred and two beast-men emerged from behind them. One looked like your run-of-the-mill wolf-man, but the other was more exotic. I guessed he was a brass demon chimera, one of Krotz's truly twisted creations.

Because they were beast-men spawned from Krotz's magic, I assumed that both were pretty much immune to offensive spells. I quickly searched my mind for a more roundabout strategy.

"It-it can't be!" I eventually cried, feigning extreme surprise.

"Heh!" the half demon chortled. "Looks like we surprised the girl."

"You can't possibly think that you two stand a chance against us, do you?!" I exclaimed. "Say it ain't so!" I clapped my hands over my mouth as the beast-men stared at each other, dumbfounded.

"H-hey!" the half demon sputtered. But he had a trick (well, two) up his sleeve, because just then he drew two blades from sheaths slung across his back: one long sword and one short.

The wolf-man didn't draw his own blade. He seemed content to simply watch the half demon face off with me.

"Didn't you hear me, bozo?" I drawled darkly. "You're seriously underestimating our power. But . . ." I shook my head and clicked my tongue. "Now that you're here, it's too late to repent. Prepare to die—and be a dear and do it quietly?"

Damn, I'm witty. Someone write that down.

"Huh!" the half demon growled. "You're quite the tough talker, ain't you?" He leered over at Xelloss and pointed a claw-tipped finger at him. "Master Balgumon said to watch out for that one. He's a real punk, I hear."

The wolf-man nodded. "Right," he said in a grating, snarling tone. "But no one said the others were weak. They may be crafty little buggers."

"W-well," the half demon stuttered, his cockiness quickly draining, "maybe." He stood there for a moment, his hands gripping his blades, but then his shoulders slumped, and his resolve visibly left him.

"Y'know," he muttered, "I don't think it's such a good idea to square off with the punk while the others are here. They're wily, I can tell."

Typical cannon fodder for you. Trash-talking one minute and whining the next.

The half demon smiled at me nervously. "I don't suppose you'd let us retreat now, would ya?"

"I might," I mused, "if you tell us where your new hideout is."

"Hmm," the half demon grunted. "Well, maybe just this—"

Seizing the moment, the wolf-man pounced, going straight for me. He still hadn't touched his sword—he was attacking with his claw!

"Hey!" I cried. They'd almost had me fooled.

Since there was no time for me to dodge the wolf-man's slash, I did the opposite: I rammed my shoulder into his abdomen to throw his attack off. The wolf-man's claw still swiped at me, but it only ripped through the mantle over my back. Unfortunately, he still managed to kick me in the gut.

"Nngh!" I grunted as I was sent hurtling across the path. When I finally stopped rolling, I looked up to see the wolf-man squaring off with Zel and Zel's broadsword.

The wolf-man growled. Stepping back to put some distance between the two of them, he finally reached behind him and drew out his own sword.

"Damn!" roared the half demon. He followed his partner's lead and charged abruptly, aiming for Amelia.

"Fireball!" she shouted.

Handy with magic as she is, her fireball hit the half demon right in the chest. The explosion sent him soaring through the air and thudding into a nearby tree.

"H-heh heh," he chuckled as he slowly picked himself up. "Fireball isn't gonna work, girlie. Not against *my* body."

Amelia ignored him. "Fireball!" she cried again, launching another.

KA-BOOM!

Again, the half demon crashed into a tree, nearly toppling it. The collision made the ground shudder. But, as before, he picked himself up off the dirt and slowly wiped the dust off his body.

"I-I told you," he panted, impatience creeping into his tone.

"Fireball!"

This time, I saw the half demon shake his head the instant before the fireball slammed him into a boulder farther away.

"Uhh," he moaned, shakily getting to his feet. "Y-you're wastin' your . . . nngh."

I stopped worrying about Amelia's well-being. Even if fireballs couldn't burn the half demon's impervious skin, constantly smashing him into nearby scenery was knocking him into a stupor.

I pushed myself up from the ground and looked over at the wolf-man. With Amelia pounding his buddy, he was left to face Zelgadiss, Xelloss, and me alone. It was a pretty lopsided match, and I almost felt sorry for the hairy jerk.

Ah, but what're you gonna do?

At the moment, the wolf-man had his hands—er, claws—tied, locking swords with Zelgadiss. Of course, not being the type of girl to sit on the sidelines while there's a rip-roaring battle underway, I licked my lips and chanted a spell. Zelgadiss must've heard me, because he took that moment to leap clear.

"Elmekia Lance!" I shouted.

The wolf-man, stuck in the path of my spell, could only blurt out a curse before diving out of the way. Lucky for him, he managed to evade my Lance.

"Stupid kids are stronger 'n they look!" he cried as he scrambled to his feet. "Retreat!" he called back to his friend as he ran into the forest. "We'll die like dogs out here!"

The half demon, suddenly panicking, ducked under Amelia's newest fireball and sprinted after his partner. "I'm too pretty to die!" he sniveled as he scurried away. I noticed that the half demon ran with a limp, obviously a result of Amelia's pummeling. I knew he wouldn't be able to escape with a bad leg if we pursued immediately.

Zelgadiss obviously realized the same thing. "Follow them!" he shouted before plunging into the forest.

Amelia, Xelloss, and I looked at each other. Xelloss shrugged, then the three of us ran after.

There wasn't a path in the woods, so we had the pleasure of tripping over every rock, root, and bush that paths are made to avoid. On the plus side, the half demon couldn't keep very far ahead with his injury, but the brush and branches slowed us down. The beast-men were lucky they'd run into the forest; had they decided to flee across open ground, we could've flown and attacked them from above.

The pursuit dragged on and on. Even Xelloss, sporting his usual grin, began to show signs of fatigue; you could see it in his dimming eyes.

This is definitely the most annoying fight we've had in a while, I thought. *And considering some of the gems we've fought, that's saying a lot.*

"Finally," Zel whispered harshly as we reached the edge of the forest. Ahead we could see the outskirts of a small, godforsaken village. Our two favorite beast-men were busy making a beeline for the center of town.

An ugly farmer with a bunch of unwashed kids in tow pulled a stupid-looking cow along. Seeing the beast-men tearing toward them, the farmer and his kids screamed and scattered. The startled cow, meanwhile, mooed frantically and started to poop all over the place in fear.

"Crap," I muttered. Those beast-men were proving to be pretty crafty. Not only could they get hostages if they wanted, but we couldn't fight them all-out in a village full of innocents. I just hoped their ugly mugs would be enough to scare the locals into hiding.

Things took an odd turn when the beast-men suddenly halted in the middle of the street that ran through the village. Alarmed and not far behind, the four of us stopped in our tracks.

The beast-men stood their ground and turned to face us. I certainly hoped they didn't want to turn the main street into a battleground.

"So you've finally come to your senses!" Amelia exclaimed, pointing a finger at our foes. "Perhaps now you realize there's no honor in evil—not now and not ever!"

"Bah!" the half demon growled, gnashing his teeth. "Where's the justice in four against two? That's *cheating*."

Amelia's hair bristled and her nostrils flared in response to the rather snide comeback. "No!" she shot back. "This is the Power of Friendship! The Power of Unity!"

Zelgadiss, Xelloss, and I simultaneously averted our eyes. *Right.*

"Whatever," the half demon muttered. "Look, we've had enough running around. Why don't we just settle this right here?"

Something was wrong. A chill ran up my spine.

"If that's what you want," Amelia declared, "then that's what you'll get!"

The half demon's lips curled into an evil grin. "Hey!" he called. "Did ya hear that, boys?"

They came crawling out of the shadows, from out of alleyways and darkened doorways, from behind horse carts and underneath wagons. By my rough count, we'd been surrounded by twenty beast-men, who all looked very ready for a fight.

Crap!

Xelloss let slip a little yelp and I turned to him abruptly. Wasn't he the relaxed one with the unnerving perma-smile? Exactly how much trouble were we in?!

"Dammit," Zelgadiss hissed. "A trap."

"Ya got that right, Rocky." The half demon cackled. "Master Krotz told us all about how strong you guys are. Even *I'd* have to go all out to slay Vedur and Gilfa. We knew there was no way two of us could stand up to the four of you."

It began to dawn on me as the half demon spoke: he and the wolf-man had only been decoys! They'd lured us into the middle of a village in the middle of *nowhere*, with the woods at our back and civilians cramping our style. We were trapped in every sense of the word.

I thought about trying something big. Since the enemy was amassed quite a ways down the street, I wondered if I had enough room to get off a Dragon Slave without destroying the town. Then again, the enemy was clearly aware of our abilities, so maybe a Dragon Slave was exactly what they wanted me to try. I decided to hold off for the moment.

If it came down to hand-to-hand combat, Zelgadiss and I were pretty smooth with our blades, but I worried about the others. Xelloss was stuck with a staff and Amelia only had her fists—not exactly a power combo.

"Sorry," came a familiar voice, "but it's probably best you don't put up a fight."

I blinked. *I heard that voice back in the mountains*, I thought as I turned to its source. A tall beast-man stood half a head over the rest, his physique a hybrid of man and white tiger. His eyes glittered with the same silver radiance as the fur that lined his face. A strangely designed suit of plate armor hugged his body, and in his hands rested a massive battleaxe.

"Um . . . Duclis?" I asked uneasily.

He gave a start. Silver eyes peered at me carefully.

"Wait," he murmured, "that's not . . . the lost little boy, is it?" He lightly grazed his cheek with the blade of his battleaxe, his face perplexed.

"You were a girl?" he asked after another moment of thinking. "Well, I suppose that makes sense. You must've been in disguise. You certainly fooled me."

I wasn't thrilled at the concept of being such a convincing boy, but this wasn't the time to argue.

"Are you all right, Mister Duclis?" the half demon asked nervously. He eyed the white tiger with skepticism.

At that, Duclis made a shooing gesture. "I'm fine," he assured his group. "No need to worry. It's just . . ." He brought his battleaxe up to his cheek again and began lightly scratching at his whiskers. "How unfortunate, you know? I'm not fond of fighting those I've become acquainted with."

Amelia leaned over to me. "Miss Lina," she whispered. "Do you know that guy?"

"I'll explain later," I replied out of the corner of my mouth. I turned my attention back to Duclis.

"Excuse me," I called. "I do have one question."

Silver eyes met mine. "Hmm?"

"Why are you guys following Krotz?" I took a breath. "The guy took away your human bodies. He worships a Demon Lord and he's trying to revive a Demon Beast as we speak. He might end up destroying the *world* for all we know!"

Duclis frowned. "I wouldn't expect you to understand, miss," he said gravely. "Almost all of us here," he gestured to the other beast-men, "were nearly dead when Master Krotz found us. I was a mercenary used as a sacrificial pawn by my own comrades; Master Krotz saved me from my wounds by transforming me into a chimera."

"Ah," Xelloss commented. "So now you're *his* pawn."

I winced at Xelloss' words. There was no beating around the bush with him.

"I understand that," Duclis replied calmly. "But I have nothing left to live for as a human, and no home to go back to. I imagine it's the same for most of these men."

Zelgadiss glared. "That puts us back to where we started," he muttered. "A fight." He slowly drew his sword.

I could tell things were about to get ugly. Hoping to avoid any *extra* problems, I leaned over and whispered to Xelloss, "Keep your flash to a minimum."

He smiled at me. "Fine," he whispered back. "I'll keep my strategy nice and simple."

I wasn't satisfied. Xelloss was still trying to squirm his way into doing extreme damage.

"Just don't use anything more lethal than we need, you get me?"

Xelloss shrugged.

With a deep sigh, Duclis proclaimed, "It's time to begin. Our conversation is wasting time."

"FIGHT!" roared the half demon, clearly ready to make the first move. He charged straight for Amelia.

Zelgadiss, however, moved in to cover her. Amelia was already chanting a spell, and I could hear what it was: Ra Tilt.

Ra Tilt only affects one foe at a time, but it's immensely lethal, even against brass demons. She wasn't wasting any time. I noticed several other beast-men suddenly advance on Amelia. Following her lead, I began chanting my own spell as I drew my short sword.

Fine. Bring it on!

Duclis slowly concealed his face with a silver-colored helm. Peering at us through the slit in his visor, he hoisted his battleaxe in one hand.

Clang!

Sparks jumped from the half demon's long sword as it clashed with Zelgadiss' blade. "You're mine!" the half demon snarled as he brandished his short sword with his other hand. He tried to slash low with the short blade, but Zel blocked it with his *palm*.

"What?!" the half demon cried out in surprise.

"Elmekia Lance!" I shouted.

My first target was Duclis himself. If I could eliminate him with a spell, that would make squaring off against the lesser beast-men—who I figured were under his leadership—a heck of a lot easier. With or without high magic resistance, I doubted he could sustain the full impact of Elmekia Lance.

But to my surprise, Duclis didn't falter a step in his oncoming charge. And to my *horror*, he took the Lance to the chest and didn't miss a beat.

What the hell?! I thought. Something was very wrong.

"Amelia!" I yelled. "Zel! Fall back!" With all my strength, I leapt as far away as I could.

"What?!" Zelgadiss shouted back. He pushed off the half demon and jumped out of the fray.

But Amelia just stood there. She kept chanting her spell, even as a beast-man reached her and raised his sword above his head.

"AMELIA!" I screamed.

In the blink of an eye, Amelia slipped out of her position and zipped behind her attacker. Without losing another moment, she slammed a vicious kick into the beast-man's back.

"Huh?" the beast-man blurted as he staggered.

I blinked. Since when could Amelia move that fast?!

Since beast-men are tough, meaty bastards, her kick hadn't done more than knock the thing off balance. But the move was lucky—the beast-man crashed into Duclis, who deflected him with his free hand. "Ugh!" Duclis grunted at him. "I told you to be careful!"

That was the moment Amelia finished her spell. "Ra Tilt!" she shouted, and a pillar of roaring blue flames enveloped Duclis.

But when the pillar vanished, Duclis was still standing there. Amelia and I gasped.

"I see," Duclis murmured. "It's true—you are talented."

"W-wha—?" The word caught in my throat. How the hell had that guy survived Ra Tilt?!

"Don't tell me my immunity to your magic surprises you." Duclis tapped his plate mail with a hairy knuckle. "It's the armor, girls. The armor Master Krotz gave me."

My heart dropped to my toes. Duclis' silver eyes glittered.

"Zanaffar's sealed inside it."

4: THE SILVER BEAST RISES AGAIN

melia and I gasped again. It was a gasp-worthy day if ever there was one.

Did he just say Zanaffar's sealed in his armor?!

"Z-Zel!" I shrieked. "You didn't say they could do that!"

"Don't get on my case!" he shot back. "How was I supposed to know?!"

He had a point. But it was still way, way too weird.

It's taking me awhile to get my head around this, folks. Excuse me for a minute.

If Zanaffar was nothing more than a deflecting suit of armor against attack-spells, that was good news for us. An evil breastplate was a lot easier to deal with than some super chimera capable of sneezing destruction on entire cities.

But right then, the gang of attacking beast-men left little time for contemplation. I figured we probably wouldn't be able to kill Duclis, but we had a chance of wiping out his buddies and then hightailing it out of there.

Gripping my sword again, I glanced over at Xelloss. He was pretty much running circles around his attackers, using his staff to parry their blades and dodging between their numbers. The man was poetry in action. The exasperated beast-men shouted things like, "Die!" and, "Stay still so I can kill you!" but it obviously didn't help. They weren't having as good a time as Xelloss was, that was for sure.

To be honest, I was a little embarrassed for the guys—all ten of them. I know *I* would hate getting my ass kicked by a guy half my size when I'd brought nine of my buddies along. I was just glad to see Xelloss was not using his magic; fried beast-man was good, fried village was not.

Amelia and I had it easier than Xelloss, but the odds against us were still three to one—*and* we were stuck with Duclis. At least none of the guys in the group compared to Vedur; I found I could go toe-to-toe with pretty much any of them.

"Yaaa!" roared an insect-headed beast-man as he charged me with his sword.

I parried his strike with my own blade. "Think again, ugly," I spat out as I pushed him off.

My goal was to back out of sword range, but the beast-man pressed in tightly and didn't give me the chance. I was contemplating what to do about that when yet another unexpected detail livened up the party.

"Nngh!" One of the beast-men grunted as an extra pair of hands emerged from his sides and brandished their very own shiny daggers.

Yes, ladies and gentlemen, I was ready to call it a day.

"Ew!" I yelled, kicking the extra-handed beast-man in the stomach and using the force of the kick to propel myself backward. Finally, the distance I needed. One of the hands had managed to slash my right foot, but it was more annoying than painful.

Handy little buggers.

After quickly ducking out of the way of another beast-man's attack, I chanted a spell.

"Oh, no you don't!" a different beast-man shouted. He ran and took a slash at me, and I barely managed to evade it.

Amelia leapt through the air and slammed her foot between the guy's eyes. He fell to the ground with a dull thud.

I threw her an appreciative glance just before releasing my spell. "Vu Vraimer!" I cried.

The ground began to shake and rumble; huge chunks of earth heaved up from a particular spot and began molding themselves into a new form. Moments later, I had a golem.

SLAYERS: THE SILVER BEAST

Vu Vraimer employs low-ranking earth spirits floating about in the air to transform hunks of ground into a possessed, controllable form. My lovely new golem was twice the size of any of my opponents.

"Wha—?!" cried a startled beast-man.

"Golem!" I commanded, enjoying the spectacle of a group of beast-men about to wet their pants. "Go!"

The golem lurched forward, swinging down its huge fist on the nearest enemy. "Ba!" it boomed.

Squish!

The beast-man slammed against the ground. Unsurprisingly, he didn't get back up.

Duclis took a step back. "Well," he said slowly, "I'm certainly impressed."

With that, he crouched and charged the golem at full speed. *Here we go*, I thought, bracing myself for the oncoming collision.

"Hang in there, golem!" I called.

"*Ba*," the golem grunted. As per my command, it wound its arm back and swung its fist in an upward arc for Duclis, who sidestepped the blow, hoisted his battleaxe high above his head, and whirled around on his heels like a top.

"Nice try!" he shouted. "But I'm afraid you're too slow!" The axe, glinting in the sun, fell on the golem with a whoosh and a clang.

BOOM!

My golem shattered into a pile of rubble and a haze of dust.

Damn.

With the golem out of service, Zelgadiss suddenly and inexplicably decided to charge straight at Duclis. I was about to call out his name and add an unflattering epithet when I realized he had a plan.

Just before slamming weapons with Duclis, Zelgadiss slipped past him in a blur and made for the half demon standing nearby. Not a bad psych-out, I had to admit.

"I saw right through that!" the half demon cackled, swinging his sword up for a slash. But Zelgadiss had one more trick up his sleeve.

"Ra Tilt!" he shouted.

As soon as the words hit the air, blue flames consumed the half demon. As his former body crumbled to the ground in a neat little pile, Zelgadiss slipped past it and cut down a dumbfounded beast-man that was watching the spectacle. Zelgadiss' sword hewed through the onlooker like a knife through butter.

Three down!

Not to be outdone, I spread my feet and began chanting my next spell. *I'll be damned if he comes out of this looking cooler than me.*

That's when the insect-headed beast-man decided to take another swing at me. I parried his strike then jerked back to avoid his kick. Blue flames engulfed him before he could regain his balance.

Amelia could be pretty handy with Ra Tilt, too.

That's four!

Just then, a bunch of the beast-men fighting Xelloss took notice of us. They snarled something to each other before running in our direction.

That's when Duclis got freaky on us.

"Hmph!" he huffed as he sent a swift kick toward Amelia. She managed to step back and evade the kick, but then Duclis planted his foot on the ground, whirled around, and—

Crash!

Amelia flew back and tumbled onto the street. I blinked in amazement.

Was that a tail?!

The instant Amelia had avoided the kick, she'd been slammed across the chest with something long and thick. I wasn't sure if the thing was Duclis' or if the Zanaffar sealed within his suit had magically lashed out.

Amelia scrambled to her feet, but I could tell the kick had knocked the wind out of her. Duclis advanced, raising his battleaxe again, just as Zelgadiss ran up from behind.

"Hmph!" huffed Duclis as he whipped around, his axe glinting.

With a severe metallic clang, Duclis cleaved Zelgadiss' broadsword clean in half.

But . . . we needed that!

I wondered if Duclis knew how to wield Zanaffar in ways we couldn't even fathom. I considered bringing my talismans into the fray, but there were still too many variables with amplification that I couldn't predict. Besides, what good would amplified powers have if my target was impervious to whatever I could throw at it?

"Damn," Zelgadiss murmured as he stared, wide-eyed, at his freshly broken sword. He turned and ran for the powdery ashes of the half demon he'd Ra Tilt-ed earlier; the dead demon's sword was half buried in his remains.

"Think again!" snarled a wolf-man who stepped into Zel's path. The wolf-man swung his sword, which Zelgadiss barely managed to parry with the broken half of his broadsword. Amelia and I were too busy with the new beast-men from Xelloss' share to help.

Zelgadiss' problems doubled when Duclis came at him from behind.

"Zel!" I yelled.

I knew Zelgadiss heard me, but he was still locked in combat with the wolf-man; he didn't have the slack to shift to Duclis, who raised his battleaxe over Zel's head.

No!

CHUNK!

Duclis grunted in surprise as the giant blade of his battleaxe went whirling away in a random direction. Duclis lowered his arms to stare at what was left of his weapon: a splintery, broken-off stick.

"What?!" cried the wolf-man, his beady little eyes darting to Duclis' destroyed axe. A streak of blazing light suddenly sliced across his chest; with a bloodcurdling howl, the wolf-man hit the dirt and proceeded to bleed all over the place.

Zelgadiss turned to his light-bearing ally. "Glad you could stop by," he remarked smartly, his rocky fist reaching up to tap at a golden blond head.

Gourry!

My exceedingly late protector smiled and gripped his Sword of Light again. "Yeah," he replied sheepishly. "Pretty good entrance, though, huh?"

It was Gourry, all right.

"You first!" Gourry cried, leaping for Duclis. Duclis, clearly in possession of a brain, hurried to retreat.

Gourry was unfazed—he simply shifted directions and began slicing through the ranks of attacking beast-men. As the chimeras screamed and fell and tripped over themselves around him, he made up for his late arrival by racking up quite a body count.

Ah, it was good to be kicking ass again.

Duclis scowled. "I won't stand for this!" he boomed as he chucked aside his sheared axe haft. He thrust his right hand high into the air.

VMMMM!

A streak of light sprang out from within his closed fist.

My jaw dropped. *Is that another Sword of Light?!* I thought frantically. Whatever it might have been, it was long, solid, and he held it like a weapon.

"This'll put a stop to you!" Duclis shouted as he charged. Gourry whipped around to confront him and brought his own blade up to parry.

The two light swords clashed . . .

. . . and Duclis' shattered into a million tiny sparks.

"What?!" Duclis cried.

Gourry didn't waste time. He swung his superior blade in a gleaming arc and sliced deeply into Duclis' chest.

That pretty much ended the battle. With Duclis reduced to a bleeding, dying wreck, the beast-man force quickly fell apart. The few that ended up surviving the next several minutes fled into the hills, leaving their dead and wounded behind.

The main street of the village had turned into a graveyard of hacked and slashed beast-man corpses. The remaining survivors included the fading Duclis; he knelt in the dirt, panting, and slowly shook his head.

"What," he breathed, "what was that . . . weapon?" He lifted up his pained face to get a better look at us. The guy obviously had no idea what had hit him.

"That," I said quietly, "was the legendary Sword of Light."

Duclis smiled weakly at my reply. "I see," he panted. "If Z-Zanaffar exists, then it should be no surprise that the Sword exists as well." He closed his eyes. "But w-what kind of weapon stands a chance against Light? That's not very . . . fair." He coughed again and blood dripped down his chin.

I shifted uneasily. *Okay, folks. Nothing to see here.*

"You're going . . . after Master Krotz?" Duclis asked.

I nodded.

"He d-drew you off. The new hideout is south of Mane . . . closer to the lake." He took a long, shaky breath. "We got ahead of you . . . using a shortcut."

"Why are you telling us this?"

Duclis shook his head. "I don't know," he replied. "Maybe because . . . I've taken . . . a liking to you?"

Yeah, *that* made me feel pretty rotten. Duclis spat out more blood and I noticed his silver eyes growing dim.

"Be careful," he whispered. "Grouj's . . . Zanaffar . . . is more powerful than . . ."

Before he could finish, Duclis fell forward onto the road with a dusty thud. He heaved one more breath then stopped breathing altogether.

Nobody said anything for a minute. When Amelia spoke at last, it was to murmur, "Did you know him?"

"Mm." I didn't have a straight answer to the question, so I just gave her a tentative shrug.

I wondered about Duclis' last words. Grouj's Zanaffar . . . Did that mean there was more than one type of Zanaffar? And was "Grouj's Zanaffar" stronger than the one in Duclis' armor?

Like one Zanaffar wasn't enough!

"So," Gourry suddenly said, breaking through my thoughts. "Everyone in one piece? Nobody missing any limbs?" He smiled at Xelloss, Zelgadiss, Amelia, and me, and then casually reached out to tousle my hair.

CRACK!

My uppercut landed squarely under his jaw. Gourry's head snapped back like one of those spring-necked dolls; it was really pretty funny.

"Wha—?!" he spluttered, grabbing his chin. "What was that for?!"

"Don't you *dare* play innocent with me!" I shrieked, ready to finally vent my anger. "Where the hell have you been all this time?!"

Gourry stroked his bruised jaw, his disheveled hair catching in his fingers. "I was looking for you and Amelia, duh."

"Oh *really*?" I snapped, my hands at my hips. "Then let me ask you this." I took a step closer. I clearly had him more than a little scared, which thoroughly satisfied me.

"Before we got separated," I grated, "I told you that Mane Village was the enemy's stronghold. Why the hell didn't you just go there? Why'd you wait to suddenly show up all the way out here?!"

Gourry blinked. "That was it!" he cried, smacking his fist into his palm. "Mane Village!"

I had the strong suspicion that his excuse was fantastically stupid.

"Look," he blurted. "After I shook off the beast-man group in the woods, I looked everywhere in the forest but couldn't find either of you. I figured I had to go back to the village where you said the group's hideout was, but . . . um . . ." He trailed off.

"Let me guess—you forgot the place's name."

He nodded somberly.

THWACK!

I whacked Gourry's face with the slipper in my hand.

"Do you have *any* idea how much trouble we went through just because *you* got *lost*?!"

"W-wait a minute!" Gourry cried, holding his palms out.

"You're not talking your way out of this one, buddy!"

"It's not that! Look, wait!" He paused, staring at the slipper in my hand. "Where the heck did you get that slipper?"

I glanced at it, then back at Gourry. "I took it out of my pocket!"

"Um, why do you have a slipper in your pocket?"

I admit it was a valid question.

"I got it at an inn awhile back," I replied shortly. "Remember? I said the slippers were nice, and that I liked nice things, so I swiped them."

"Nice things?" he repeated.

A long, awkward silence hung between us. I couldn't think of a comeback.

"Um, Lina," Amelia offered at last, "this isn't exactly the time for a lovers' quarrel."

I whipped around to her, my eyes blazing and my cheeks red. "Who're you calling LOVERS?!" I roared.

"Let's get back to Duclis," she suggested, ignoring my rage. "He said something about Krotz's hideout being somewhere south of Mane, right? Somewhere near a lake."

Before I could reply, Xelloss took a step back. "Yes," he said politely. "And that marks my exit. Thank you for the memories, everyone." He bowed graciously then turned to leave.

We stared dumbly at his back. "H-hey, wait!" Amelia called. "Where are you going?"

Xelloss glanced back with his cool, unchanging smile.

"Don't misunderstand," he said quietly. "Though you and Zelgadiss are comrades, I am merely not your enemy."

Silence. His smile had never looked creepier.

"Until now, Master Krotz had rather significant forces at his command—and I did not know the location of his new hideout, as you did not." His gaze fell on Zelgadiss. "But that is no longer the case. You must remember that my objective is the Claire Bible, and I have no intention of handing the manuscript over to Mister Zelgadiss, just as he has no intention of handing it over to me."

Zelgadiss paused. "That depends on the contents of it," he said after a moment, his tone noticeably sullen.

Xelloss nodded slightly. "In other words," he noted, "we've become competitors, and our continued collaboration has therefore become mutually counter-productive. Don't you agree that it's better to part at this juncture?"

When none of us answered, he shrugged. "Then I shall be off."

He made a blessing motion as he turned, then calmly walked away. We watched him go, dazed and uncomfortable, until he vanished around a bend in the winding path ahead.

"Hey!" I called out. "Hey, hold on!"

I found myself suddenly running after him, out of the village, stopping only at the bend in the path where I'd seen him turn. But there was nobody there. All I saw was an empty trail bordered by thick groves of trees winding its way along the foot of the hills.

After a while, I heard the faint crunch of footsteps behind me. I turned to see Zelgadiss.

Silently, he gazed in the direction Xelloss had gone. After a moment, his eyes shifted to me and I saw something very dark hanging behind his pupils.

"It's possible," he murmured, his voice grave, "that *he* may prove the most difficult opponent of all."

***

It took another two days to get back to Mane, since we had to travel through villages, mountain passes, and pathless forests to get there. By the time we arrived, we were *six* days behind Krotz and extremely cranky. It didn't take long after that to reach the lake Duclis had mentioned; it was just south of Mane, and we were anxious to get the party started.

We crouched behind some bushes and held a strategy session. An ancient building stood not far from our hiding place, likely another remnant from the age of Letidius. As with the first hideout we'd blown the crap out of a week or so before, we didn't notice any guards patrolling the building. Krotz either didn't believe in security or he was setting us up.

"I think it's pretty safe to assume that Krotz is hurting from his recent losses," Zelgadiss said in a low voice. He sighed, peering through the concealing plant life at the compound that loomed ahead. "Of course, that could be even more reason for him to spring a trap."

Gourry shrugged. "We've still gotta go in," he pointed out. "Trap or no trap."

I was suddenly struck by a brilliant idea. I beckoned them closer.

"How about this?" I whispered. "First, we get Gourry to charge in on a suicide mission. If he doesn't come back out after a little while, we assume he's dead and start lobbing Dragon Slaves into their hideout."

"Okay!" Amelia flashed a thumbs-up.

"Sounds good to me," Zelgadiss agreed.

Gourry sighed.

Before you start judging me, we all needed a tension breaker and Gourry had done the least work. We were only kidding! Well . . . half kidding.

After we finished having a chuckle at Gourry's expense, I got serious. "We won't be able to use very big offensive spells inside," I murmured. "Everyone understand that?"

They nodded. I was about to continue when I heard the fireball.

FWOOOM!

A flaming sphere arced toward us and detonated, its red-and-orange plume expanding as it exploded. Of course, by then the four of us had figured out what was happening and had long since scattered.

Five figures in flowing red robes stood nearby. Four of them, based on their hulking frames, were obviously beast-men. The fifth looked suspiciously like . . .

Not him *again!*

"I regret to inform you that trespassing here will not be tolerated," declared Balgumon.

Amelia shook a fist. "So," she called, loud and clear. "The evil cult's sub-leader has finally come out to face justice!"

"There is neither justice nor evil among humans," Balgumon retorted shortly, "only weakness and strength. But life forms as low as yourselves—vulgar vermin that you are— are incapable of understanding that." With that, he narrowed his eyes, swept his robe aside, and charged.

Straight at Gourry.

For a second, I thought it was a joke. As the skinny, pasty little man ran at our hulking swordsman, I wondered if Balgumon was insane. What sorcerer in his right mind physically charges someone three times his weight?

Suddenly, something silver flashed from Balgumon's hands.

"Ow!"

To my surprise, the sound came from *Gourry*. As I watched, Gourry doubled up from the force of the blow and staggered back a few steps.

What the hell?!

Balgumon clutched two swords in his hands. My brain skipped over the ridiculousness of it for a second, then quickly tried to process. Had he hit Gourry? With double blades? Gourry's sword skill was pretty much the best I'd ever seen, and Balgumon didn't look strong enough to *lift* two swords, let alone wield them.

I'd always just assumed, considering Balgumon's skinny arms and robe-intensive wardrobe, that the guy was a sorcerer. But Balgumon was a *swordsman*.

"I know of Duclis' failure!" he shouted, slashing his blades to and fro. "I know that it was he who informed you of our location. I also know that you bear a most troublesome sword!" Balgumon jabbed, whirled, and pressed in on Gourry, his robes twirling around him as he moved. "However," he sneered, "if I give you no opportunity to draw your blade, I'll be no danger at all!"

Balgumon was frightening in action. He moved so quickly that the blades in his hands became just blurs of motion; I could barely keep track of him as he and Gourry bounded from one spot to another. Don't get me wrong—Gourry kept pace with his opponent's lightning-quick movements just fine, but Balgumon stayed right in Gourry's face and refused to give him the distance he needed to draw the Sword of Light.

I would have liked to give Gourry a hand, but Amelia, Zelgadiss, and I were a little preoccupied: the four beast-men had pounced on us like flies on you-know-what.

Even if I hadn't been busy with my own fight, there would've still been very little I could do for Gourry. My skill with a sword wasn't nearly good enough to face Balgumon, and the fight was too close for me to cast a spell and not kill them both.

Unless I can create a distraction . . .

"Amelia!" I shouted as I parried an incoming beast-man's blade with my short sword. "Zel! Buy me some time—I'm gonna blow up their hideout with a Dragon Slave!"

Hearing that, Balgumon screeched to a halt. "W-what?!" he stammered.

The momentary pause was enough for Gourry to take a giant leap backward and finally get some space. But before they could continue their battle, they were interrupted.

KA-BOOOOOM!

There was no mistaking it. It was the sound of an explosion—a very *big* one—from within the cult's compound. *And I didn't even do anything*, I marveled.

Balgumon looked visibly shocked. "What?!" he exclaimed. "What's the meaning of this?!"

Balgumon hurriedly backed away from Gourry and scanned our group. It didn't take long for him to realize that one of us was notably absent.

"Where is he?!" he cried. "Where's that infuriating priest?!"

Xelloss. If the explosion was actually his doing, then he had excellent timing.

Balgumon glared at us. "So that was your plan, you . . . !" He was too busy sprinting toward his hideout to finish whatever insult he had in mind. The beast-men watched him go, looked confusedly at each other, and then scurried off behind him.

"Master Balgumon?" I heard one of them squeak as they disappeared into the building.

We'd caught a lucky break, it seemed. And Zelgadiss wanted to take full advantage of it.

"Let's go!" he yelled.

At his signal, we followed Balgumon and the four beast-men into the hideout.

***

"Damn," Zelgadiss muttered under his breath. With his foot, he carefully rolled over the beast-man corpse lying just inside the building's entranceway.

The beast-man had probably been on guard duty. He couldn't have been very good-looking alive, but his death almost seemed like a cruel joke on his appearance—his head had been blown off, and pieces of it were smeared across the floor and splattered against the walls.

I knew that run-of-the-mill magic spells didn't work on Krotz's beast-men, so whoever had killed the guy had a special set of powers under his belt. If it *was* Xelloss, then I wished I knew what his secret was. Amelia obviously wondered the same thing.

"What's his technique?" she murmured.

"I don't know." Zelgadiss frowned. "I've never seen it firsthand."

Personally, I'd only seen Xelloss' skills on two occasions: the amplified Blast Bomb when we'd first met and the giant gale back in the village. How the hell did he do what he did?

"Anyway," I suggested, shaking my head, "let's just go. We're wasting time here."

We stood in a small room with only one exit: a small doorway directly across from the entrance to the outside. The doorway was open, so we could see the long, downward-sloping corridor beyond it. From the look of things, the place was a fairly large and elaborate subterranean structure.

The passageway was warm, its walls hot to the touch and largely scorched. As we proceeded down the corridor, our senses straining for any sign of a trap, we heard a continuous clatter of footsteps and the occasional rumble of explosions from deeper within. Every room along the corridor lacked a complete door and radiated heat and smoke, as if it had just been set afire. We obviously followed in the wake of a very destructive spell-caster—one who went a bit overboard with the fireballs.

"Damn him," Zelgadiss growled as we took in the carnage. "What the hell is that nutcase thinking?"

Xelloss had obviously wanted to cause as much confusion and alarm among Krotz's forces as possible. It seemed to me that he was being awfully stupid about it, considering that we were searching for an ancient and probably highly flammable manuscript.

BOOOOOM!

Yet another explosion, this time much closer.

We're catching up!

"This way!" I called to the others, breaking into a run down the passage. A lone figure, silhouetted against the flickering wall lights, suddenly crossed our path.

Balgumon.

The four of us stopped in our tracks and prepared to fight—or, more likely, start a fight and then get interrupted in the middle of it—but he barely paused to acknowledge us.

"Curses," he hissed before darting away down a nearby side corridor. Obviously, there was something on his mind that took precedence over dealing with us.

Something more important than dealing with us? That sounded like just where we wanted to be.

"After him!" I shouted, and we all chased the man. He reached a door ahead of us, dove inside, and managed to lock it before we could get there.

"It won't open," Gourry grunted as he tried the knob. "It's locked."

Thank you, Gourry!

"Out of the way," Amelia ordered. As she began chanting a spell, Gourry, Zelgadiss, and I quickly left what would shortly become a blast radius.

"Dam Brass!"

CR-RACK!

Amelia's spell not only shattered the door, but also destroyed the doorframe and a lot of the wall around it. We peeked through our newly created hole and into what looked like a small chapel.

The interior of the chapel looked like it had recently been altered. The statues of old gods on pedestals had been hacked off, and on a small altar in the center of the room stood a statue of Ruby Eye Shabranigdu. It wasn't a particularly accurate statue, though; the real thing was uglier.

At the opposite end of the chapel was another door. That's where we spotted Balgumon, fiddling around with its lock.

"So *this* is where you're hiding the manuscript," I growled. The four of us stalked toward him, trying to look as menacing as possible.

The lock under Balgumon's hands opened. He turned to us, a triumphant smile on his thin lips, and pulled open the door.

A shadowy form blocked his escape route. Balgumon's expression went from confident to terrified in an instant.

"You!" he shouted.

As far as last words go, his was pretty unimpressive.

Splonk!

With a sound like a ripe tomato being violently popped, Balgumon's head burst off his body. The grizzly missile flew a surprising distance across the room, splattering the Demon Lord's statue with an appropriately gruesome red.

Balgumon body's remained balanced on its legs for several seconds, then unceremoniously collapsed in a heap like yesterday's laundry.

Xelloss stepped out of the doorway. He clutched a single sheet of yellowing paper in his hand.

"Hmm," he hummed as he stepped over the headless corpse and into the room. He studied the page for a while, ignoring everything else, then finally looked up.

"A page from the manuscript," he said with a satisfied nod. "No question about it. Let me thank you for the diversion you provided; it came in quite handy as I searched for this."

That's when I realized his strategy behind fireballing the place left and right. Xelloss knew that any attack on the enemy was an attack on the manuscript, so if the enemy felt threatened, their first priority would be to protect it—which also meant leading any observers right to it. Still, it had been a dangerous gamble; he could've easily set fire to the manuscript by accident during his first attack.

Zelgadiss, for the first time since I'd met him, actually seemed to lose his nerve. "Would you . . . please hand that over?" he asked quietly.

Xelloss shook his head. "Can't do that," he answered. "Even this incomplete piece is far too important."

No one dared take a step toward Xelloss. We had no idea what method he'd used to kill Balgumon, but whatever he'd done had finished the guy abruptly and gruesomely. None of us had any intention of learning his secret firsthand.

Xelloss seemed to notice the troubled look on my face, because he leaned toward me.

"Ah, Miss Lina," he said, gently but ominously. "You seem so concerned. You're wondering how I intend to use this, are you not?"

Well, since you brought it up . . .

My stomach churning, I slowly nodded.

Xelloss crumpled up the piece of manuscript in his hand. "This," he said simply, and the parchment burst into flames.

My mouth opened, but whatever I'd hoped to say died in my throat. We all watched, morbidly rapt, as the invaluable manuscript became a worthless pile of ash before our very eyes.

That's when it came to me. The rumor of someone burning a copy of the manuscript in the Kingdom of Dils.

"Y-YOU!" Zelgadiss shrieked.

Xelloss' serene expression remained unchanged. "Misfortune befalls those who use technology that they don't understand." He then casually spun around and vanished through the doorway.

Zelgadiss was still in a state of shock. "W-why that—!" he stuttered, too mortified to form a coherent thought. "I can't believe he—!"

Zelgadiss made a sudden move to pursue Xelloss, but then froze.

We heard someone approaching the doorway Xelloss had just gone through. Before we could even think of an escape, Krotz and two beast-men appeared, the three of them cloaked in their ominous red.

As Krotz passed through the doorway, his gaze fell on the corpse at his feet.

"Ba—!" he cried in a strangled voice. He fell to his knees and touched the headless, red-robed figure. "Balgumon!"

It wasn't hard to figure out that the corpse was Balgumon, even without the head. The red robes, the markings on it, and the gaunt physique all gave him away.

Krotz knelt there for a moment, his lips parted in shock, then darted his grief-stricken eyes up to glare daggers at us.

"It was you!" he exclaimed, pointing very rudely. "You did this to Balgumon!"

I shook my head. "Get over it, Krotch," I snapped. "It was *not* us. The guy you just saw leave through that door"—I pointed it out to him—"he was the one who did it."

But Krotz kept his hateful gaze fixed on me, unconvinced, as he rose to his feet. "An abominable lie," he hissed. "We saw no one leave through here."

Why am I not surprised?

"What has become of the manuscript?" he demanded.

I shrugged my shoulders in response. What was I supposed to tell him? That the parchment was turned to toast by the same guy he didn't see?

"Very well," Krotz said slowly. "Vileus! Rudia!"

The beast-men flanking him stepped forward in military unison. "Sir!"

"Go awaken Grouj!"

The beast-men gasped and glanced at each other with horror-stricken faces.

"M-Master Krotz!" cried the one named Vileus, trembling. "We mustn't!"

"That isn't Grouj anymore," Rudia whimpered. "If we aren't careful . . ."

It was unsettling to see two huge, fearsome beast-men so terrified at running what seemed like a simple errand. I figured that the Grouj character had to be one frightening guy.

Krotz turned away from the beast-men and began scanning us with his withering look. Then he pointed to us and addressed them again.

"Fine, you sniveling fools! Hold them off here, and I will awaken Grouj by my own hand!" He stomped back through the doorway and disappeared.

"Master Krotz!" Vileus entreated. The two beast-men stared after him with completely stunned expressions. After a moment, they both made for the door.

"Hold it, you two!" I shouted. It was my chance to get the whole scoop, so I squared my shoulders and tried to sound as tough as I could. "What the *hell* is going on here?"

"Silence!" Rudia snapped, glaring at me. "You've no right to speak—"

Vileus quieted him with a raised hand. "You," he said, looking our way. "You're the ones who slew Duclis, are you not?"

Gourry nodded. "Tiger guy?" he asked. "Yeah, that was us."

Vileus considered the fact for a moment, then said, "Come this way."

Nice!

Rudia's jaw dropped. "Vileus!"

Vileus ignored his comrade. When he reached the doorway, he paused to glare back at me.

"Are you going to follow or not?"

"Sure," I replied casually. "Let's go. We can talk on the way."

I approached the beast-men without hesitation, not wanting to give them the impression that I was nervous or suspicious. "Miss Lina!" Amelia cried, but I ignored her warning plea.

I followed the beast-men down the corridor. Although I tried to exude all the confidence I could muster, I was still relieved to note that Zelgadiss, Gourry, and Amelia kept in step not far behind me.

"Let me get to the point," Vileus said as he strode down the passageway. "I want you to deal with Grouj." He paused for a moment. "Or rather . . . Zanaffar."

"But isn't Zanaffar just a piece of armor with magic sealed inside?" I asked.

"I don't know all the details," he grunted, quickening his pace. "But all I know for sure is that Grouj started acting strangely soon after he began wearing that armor."

Grouj . . . Grouj . . . I realized that was the name Duclis had told me before he died. And hadn't someone mentioned him during our first attack on the cult?

Vileus continued: "Master Krotz told us that the armor assimilates its wearer and then begins to grow. He said the worst that can happen is that the wearer's mind will become a little unstable."

Hang on now; back up!

"Did you say it begins to *grow*?!" I blurted. "So the Zanaffar-sealed armor is alive?!"

Vileus nodded grimly. "So it seems."

I glanced over at my three companions. While Gourry looked as lost as usual, Zelgadiss seemed absorbed in thought and Amelia's lips tightened with worry.

"Master said that, to be on the safe side, he was putting Grouj to sleep until he stabilized." Vileus' voice became a low hiss. "But I don't think that *thing* is Grouj anymore."

Between his head-shaking and his nervous breathing, it was obvious that something had really freaked the guy out.

"Before that," Vileus continued, "Grouj had a number of . . . episodes. From time to time, he completely lost his mind. Once, he even went berserk without warning; he ended up killing quite a few people."

"Master Krotz told us it was nothing to worry about," Rudia tentatively added. He cast a quick glance at Vileus, who reacted to the remark with a snort.

"Listen," Vileus growled, his brows furrowed as he leaned closer, "Zanaffar is complete. I overheard Master Krotz announce it yesterday. I think he wants to awaken it immediately!"

Rudia's eyes widened. "But that's—"

"Think about it," Vileus interrupted. "If the armor lives and grows, then what is it *feeding* on that allows it to grow?"

Not something I want to think about.

"Are you telling me," I asked slowly, "that Zanaffar is feeding on the flesh of whoever wears it?"

Everyone gasped, except Gourry. He was observing a crack in the wall.

He turned to us. "Did something happen?" he asked. "Sorry, I think I missed it."

GOURRY!

"*Zanaffar,*" I grated, using every ounce of my will to not murder him, "is a type of parasite, apparently. It starts in a suit of armor that protects the host's body, but then it slowly consumes the host's flesh in order to grow. When the host's body is entirely consumed, Zanaffar is complete."

Gourry stared at me, and we all waited for the information to process. Finally, he came to a conclusion.

"I still don't get it."

Where's my slipper?! I need my Gourry-beating slipper!

After a few moments of seething fury, I burst out with a fast, hard, extended metaphor.

"Okay! Pretend that Zanaffar's a sketchy guy who sweet-talks a girl—that's Grouj—by saying things like, 'I'll always be there for you' and 'I'll take care of you forever' and all that.

But then, after he's won her trust, he eats her food, steals her money, and kicks her out of her own house!" I threw my arms up. "You get it now?!"

Slowly, Gourry began to nod. "I think so. Sorta."

Good enough!

Gourry put his hands on his hips. "So we just have to kill this guy, right?"

Someone please *get him out of my face!*

I swallowed my rage and forced myself back on track. "What about Duclis?" I asked Vileus. "Did he know about Zanaffar? About how it fed and grew?"

"As far as I can guess," Vileus replied somberly. "He must have known what would happen to him when he volunteered to 'bear' the second Zanaffar."

"In any case," Rudia interjected, "I have one request. When you finish off Zanaffar, do not harm Master Krotz."

I wanted to tell him to piss off, but Amelia cut in. "You guys sure do make a lot of demands!" she accused.

"What do you mean by that?!" Rudia snapped, lurching toward her.

I decided to intercede before things descended into really stupid violence.

"Look," I said flatly. "We can't make any promises. If we go after Zanaffar, I'm sure that Krotz will use any means necessary to keep us from ruining his plan." I shook my head. "If you dance close to the fire, you're gonna get burned, know what I'm saying?"

While Rudia mulled that over, possibly trying to figure out what fire dancing had to do with battling Zanaffar, the ground beneath us began to tremble. The beast-men crouched low, expecting something.

"We're too late," Rudia moaned.

The rumbling only lasted a few moments, then an ominous calm settled over the building. The beast-men urged us to run for the surface, so the six of us sprinted through the corridors and made our way outside via the quickest possible route. Soon enough, we found an exit and emerged into the daylight.

Everything looked just as calm and peaceful as when we'd arrived; the only sound I could hear was the wind rustling in the trees. The scenery had a distinct lack of world-destroying chimera monsters.

"Nothing's happening," Amelia said.

"Maybe he just farted in his sleep," Gourry suggested. "That can happen."

None of us were willing to dignify that with a response.

A few more uneventful minutes passed. Zelgadiss, finally fed up, strode angrily over to Vileus.

"Hey!" he yelled at the beast-man, "is this some kind of a game?" He unsheathed his blade and pointed it at the motionless Vileus. "Did you make all that garbage up about Zanaffar just to buy time for Krotz? You did, didn't you?!"

Instead of answering, the beast-man looked across at the hideout's entranceway.

"If only that were so," Vileus whimpered. "You may have beaten Duclis, but do not underestimate what Zanaffar can do once he is unleashed."

At that instant—

VMMMM!

A streak of light ripped across our view of the lake.

The Laser Breath!

There was no question about it—it was the exact same light that shot at us the night we fled from the cult's first hideout, only now it was *way* meaner. The beam had emerged from beneath the ground, ripped through the earth, and hit the lake with such force that the water boiled, hissed, and sprayed violently in all directions. The vaporized water created a cloud of mist over the entire area.

"GRAAAAAAAA!"

An ear-splitting roar shook the ground under our feet. In front of the hideout's entrance, a giant, gaping hole had opened in the earth.

"It's coming," I heard someone squeak.

Then again, that might have been me; I was definitely freaked out enough. As I watched, an enormous silver claw emerged from the hole and pierced the earth around the rim. The claw scraped for a moment, then the creature slowly dragged himself out into the daylight.

It was the Silver Beast—Zanaffar!

The thing was *huge*. He stood on four legs, but the more I stared at him the less I could discern what sorts of creatures his various parts had originated from. The only thing obvious about him was his head; it was clearly like that of a silver-maned wolf.

The wolf-headed, four-legged, dragon-sized beast scanned the area with his glittering eyes. Whip-like tentacles thrashed from his silver torso.

I wanted nowhere near those hideous things.

"Master Krotz!" Rudia cried meekly.

"Master Krotz?" Vileus joined in, calling in the direction of the hole. "Are you all right down there?"

The Beast craned his head in our direction.

VMMMMM!

We all screamed and scattered as the Laser Breath shot through. The beam crystallized the sand and scorched a trench-like scar in the earth.

Even scarier was what happened next: the Demon Beast charged straight at us! He fired another Laser Breath, jogging behind it, when suddenly—

Gourry deflected it.

Zanaffar halted in his tracks, stunned as his one-shot, one-kill attack swept through the earth at an angle away from his target. Gourry, his feet spread and the Sword of Light blazing in his hand, silently waited.

I saw realization dawn in those giant silver eyes. Zanaffar, his teeth bared under silver lips, made a low and cautious growl.

That's when I noticed something. Near the Demon Beast's right flank, a pathetically small figure crept over to the monster. On closer inspection, I realized it was Rudia, who was taking advantage of Zanaffar's distracted state to sneak up for a surprise attack.

I had no idea what Rudia intended, but there was no way in hell anything he could do would hurt the Beast. I wanted to yell at him to back away, but I knew that would just draw Zanaffar's attention to him and get Rudia killed even faster. I was forced to watch the beast-man's defining moment of stupidity.

The moment he was close enough, Rudia swung down his blade with everything he had.

Clang!

The sword recoiled with a hard metallic sound, knocking Rudia off balance. He hadn't even marked Zanaffar's hide.

"Damn!" Rudia shouted as he caught himself and tried to leap behind a rock.

Too late.

One of Zanaffar's silver tentacles shot out of nowhere and skewered the beast-man clean through. Rudia's body convulsed a few times, then hung there, limp. The tentacle flicked once and discarded the beast-man's corpse as if it were a dirty tissue.

Zanaffar had managed to do all this without once taking his eyes off Gourry. The Demon Beast was completely and utterly lethal.

Slowly, carefully, Zanaffar began to advance.

Gourry wasn't one for careful deliberation. Without sparing another second, he launched himself toward the Demon Beast.

"Don't approach recklessly!" Vileus shouted. But it didn't matter—Gourry was already in too deep to stop and too clueless to know any better.

Holding aloft the Sword of Light, he deflected another onslaught of the Laser Breath and closed the gap between himself and the Demon Beast. "Haa!" Gourry cried, swinging at Zanaffar's front foot.

But Zanaffar wasn't only extremely tough, he was extremely *fast*. Gourry swung, but he sliced through nothing but air. Zanaffar had avoided the attack by jumping straight up!

It surprised me how high Zanaffar's jump carried him. His enormous body became a tiny shape silhouetted against the sun, hung high in the air for a moment, and then plummeted downward—straight for Gourry. As he dropped, the Demon Beast shot a nonstop succession of Laser Breaths; Gourry had his hands full deflecting Zanaffar's attacks, robbing him of the time he needed to dodge the Beast himself.

I scrambled for a rescue plan, but Amelia was already on it.

"Fireball!" she shouted.

FWOOM!

The ball of flame arced up and slammed into the Demon Beast. It didn't do any damage, but it did manage to push him off course.

The Demon Beast landed heavily a short distance away, his impact with the earth shaking us all. The instant his claws dug into the ground again, he let loose with another salvo of Laser Breaths, all of which Gourry deflected.

I decided it was time to let loose with some magic myself.

"Blast Bomb!" I shouted.

It was one of the spells I'd been working on with my newly amplified magic. As far as I knew, I was only the third

person in the history of the world to actually cast it: the legendary sorcerer who invented it; Xelloss; and now that I had Xelloss's talismans, me. Even in Sairaag, at the height of its power, I doubted that there were any sorcerers able to cast such a powerful spell. My plan in unleashing Blast Bomb was to raise Zanaffar's surface temperature above what his hide was able to tolerate.

The Blast Bomb exploded very impressively and right on target. But when the smoke cleared, the Demon Beast wasn't fazed at all.

Hey!

There still wasn't a scratch on his shiny, silver hide. I'd never seen skin so tough in my life.

Fine, I thought quickly. *Time for a new plan.* It was clear that applying heat to the Demon Beast's body wouldn't damage it; I doubted that cold would have any effect, either. I considered trying to get around his impenetrable hide by launching a fireball straight into his mouth, but he moved too fast and released way too many Laser Breaths for me to get a clear shot. Add to that the fact that he didn't seem the least bit interested in anyone but Gourry; despite our spells, the Beast hadn't even glanced in our direction.

Gourry tried to outmaneuver Zanaffar by sliding along the Beast's massive flank, but he didn't have much luck. Zanaffar was just as quick as Gourry, so he twisted his body as much as was necessary to keep Gourry firmly in front.

"Dammit," Zelgadiss snarled. "He doesn't even have to look at us."

Amelia threw up her hands in frustration. "He doesn't have to *bother* with us," she pointed out. "And why should he, right? That Sword of Light is the only thing that can kill him."

That's when the thought hit me, like a thunderbolt out of the blue. "Maybe it is," I mumbled, "and maybe it isn't."

"What do you mean by that?"

But I didn't reply to Zelgadiss' question; I had some serious chanting to do. I had one spell in mind that, with the aid of my talismans, could possibly get Zanaffar's attention. It was a spell for summoning darkness and converging it into the shape of a blade.

Sounds cool, huh?

I'd tested out the spell several days earlier and found its destructive potential to be, for lack of a better word, *ginormous.* Of course, I hadn't deployed the spell in real combat, but it was still a hell of a spell. Powerful enough to give the Sword of Light a run for its money.

I knew it would be difficult to pull off, since the blade that the spell formed was only the size of a short sword. The spell also consumed magic energy while it was being cast, which meant that even if I used *all* my magic power, I still couldn't keep it going for very long before it burned out or my body did. Once activated, all my physical energy would go into the spell and leave me little mobility for dodging incoming attacks. My only hope was a surprise attack—a fatal, single blow, so he couldn't live to retaliate and make me very dead.

By the way, the spell I had in mind falls within the realm of what fuddy-duddies call "forbidden sorcery." It's true that it originates from the same source as my most secret of spells, the Giga Slave, and that that source just happens to be the Lord of Nightmares. Okay, so maybe the "forbidden" tag is there for a good reason. Cut me some slack—I was going up against a Demon Beast!

On the plus side, I knew it was easier to control than the Giga Slave, so I didn't foresee any (serious) problems keeping it reined in. The only problem, really, was that there was no guarantee it would hurt the Beast at all.

I hoped we could lop off one of Zanaffar's feet first, since I knew that would slow the thing down and seriously help me out. Gourry seemed to be thinking the same thing, but he wasn't having much luck getting close.

"Argh!" he cried. In a rare display of rage, Gourry scowled and charged forward with a curse. Unfortunately, Zanaffar sent a swirl of lashing tentacles out to meet him.

"Outta my way!" Gourry fumed as he moved to slash the tentacles. The moment he tried, streaks of light sprang from the tentacles' tips.

What?!

I don't think Gourry expected it, either. Despite his acrobatic ducking and the deflections of his sword, one of the streaks caught the side of his thigh; he cried out in pain and rolled across the ground.

I remembered just then how Duclis—wearing his Zanaffar-sealed suit of armor—had summoned light out of his bare hands. It had probably been an application of the Laser Breath—and that meant the tentacles' shots were, too.

Gourry grunted, tried to get up, and promptly slumped to his knees. Zanaffar laughed in his low, growling voice.

"Warrior of the Sword of Light," he boomed, "it seems you have taken this *mere beast* too lightly!"

My jaw dropped. The thing talked!

"He can communicate using human speech?!" I heard Vileus cry from somewhere.

"I have consumed my host, Grouj," Zanaffar explained with a wicked snarl, "as well as his knowledge and experience. Is it so mysterious that I am capable of communicating in your human tongue?"

He fixed his glittering, wolfish eyes on Gourry. "You indeed have treated this *mere beast* with disrespect. You underestimate my deadliness even more than the hosts I consumed."

He growled and crouched lower on his haunches. "Now set your sword aside," he ordered. "If you do, your lives shall be spared. Consuming you is of no use to me, for the defensive capability that protects me from magic denies me the power to use magic myself."

Really? I thought. So the astral seal interfered with spells both ways—it gave protection against incoming attack spells, but then prevented Zanaffar from casting his own. I wondered how Zanaffar had come to know that. Grouj wouldn't have possessed such extensive knowledge on astral seals. Krotz would've, but . . .

Wait a sec!

"What's all this about?" Zelgadiss shouted. "Is your goal to destroy the world?!"

The Demon Beast turned a bored glance in his direction. "Not particularly," he replied. "I wish merely to add to my kind. That lit sword, though it may inflict minor wounds to my flesh, is nothing but a mild hindrance."

"Add to your kind?" I asked. I crossed my arms and narrowed my eyes. "And how exactly do you plan on doing that by yourself?"

The Demon Beast had that one covered. "I shall make followers of those humans who seek power," he bellowed. "There are many humans who seek strength and will even worship Demon Lords to attain it. I shall command such a group to create more Zanaffars. It won't be difficult, as I know the procedure."

"What?!" Vileus broke in. He gripped his sword and began trembling with anger. "W-what did you do to Master Krotz?!"

Zanaffar smiled wickedly. "I," he drawled, "consumed *him* also."

Wow! Eating someone *that* important. That's hard-core.

Vileus wasn't too happy to hear that. The rage boiled up inside him 'til the lid just flipped.

"DIE!" he roared, raising his sword. He charged Zanaffar with a passionate war cry.

Um, hello?! Use your brain, doofus!

"Hey!" I yelled. "You're just gonna get yourself killed!"

But by the time the words came out, it was already too late.

ZAP!

The tentacles unleashed their deadly streaks of light. Vileus was promptly seared in half; his top and bottom portions divided evenly and thumped to the ground like hunks of ham.

Ew.

"I will say this once," the Demon Beast declared, a little too late for Vileus. "I will not hesitate to slay those who defy me." His eyes fixed on Gourry again. "Make your choice. Set aside the sword, and you may leave this place alive."

The situation only left me with one option: to give my crazy plan a shot. I wasn't too keen on ending up as pork roast *or* living in a world full of Zanaffars.

I leaned in close to Amelia and Zelgadiss and laid out my plan. "All right, guys. Listen up."

A few moments later, Zanaffar turned his head to Amelia and me. He'd noticed Amelia grab hold of me and take to the air with Levitation.

"Hmm," Zanaffar rumbled. "You've wisely chosen to run away." He turned his attention back to Gourry. "Now. Give me the sword and—"

"Gourry!" Zelgadiss interrupted. "Pass!" He jumped up and down and flailed his arms.

Gourry understood instantly. He hurled the Sword—its column of light still blazing—to Zelgadiss.

"What?!" Zanaffar roared. He had a reason to be mad—after all, it was the Sword he was afraid of, not Gourry.

"Run!" Zelgadiss ordered. Gourry got himself up on one leg and stumbled off the battlefield, dragging his wounded limb behind him.

Zanaffar's lips curled with hate. "Humans are such stupid creatures!" he snarled. With a deafening howl, he shot a beam of Laser Breath straight for Zelgadiss.

Zelgadiss somersaulted out of the way, the Sword of Light still clutched in his hand. With Zanaffar thus distracted, Amelia and I had managed, in the meantime, to float directly over him. I'd also finished chanting the amplification spell.

Let's do some damage!

Zelgadiss dropped to one knee and slammed his hand against the ground. "Dug Haut!" he shouted, and the earth began to ripple.

"Fool!" Zanaffar roared, bracing himself while the ground beneath him rumbled. "What do you think you're—"

Before Zanaffar could finish his words, the entire area under his feet collapsed.

BOOOOM!

The spell had caused Krotz's one-time hideout to crumble under Zanaffar's feet. Huge plumes of dust and smoke choked the air below Amelia and me, so we covered our mouths and waited.

When the air did clear, we could see the Demon Beast slumped in the earth—unharmed, of course, but restricted. Zelgadiss looked over the rim of the hole to inspect the damage. Even with his legs buried in rubble, Zanaffar abruptly arched his head up and sent another furious stream of Laser Breaths at Zelgadiss. Zel, smart boy that he is, ducked back behind the rim.

It was time to make my move.

> . . . *Sword of cold and darkness,*
> *Free yourself from the heavens' bonds;*
> *Become one with my power, one with my body,*
> *And let us walk the path of destruction together.*
> *Power that can smash even the souls of the gods . . .*

"Ragna Blade!"

At my call, a jet-black blade of darkness formed in my clenched hand. Exhaustion suddenly dragged at me (That spell takes a lot out of you.) I knew I couldn't keep it up long, so I had to make it count.

I gave Amelia a quick nod as a signal to let me go. I looked down in my freefall and saw my target directly below me—Zanaffar's hulking, ugly back. I braced myself for impact.

"GRUAAAAAAAAAAAAAA!" Zanaffar roared as I plunged the blade of darkness deep into his hide.

YES!

The sword sliced through Zanaffar's flesh easily—so easily, in fact, that both my arms plowed through the wound right up to the elbows. While the thrust didn't quite kill Zanaffar, it sure as hell hurt and confused him. Grimacing with pain, he craned his head around. If *I* saw a girl with her arms lodged in a gaping wound in my back, I'd be confused, too.

"Y-you!" he roared, his silver mane bristling. "What have you done?!"

By then I had already released Ragna Blade and begun chanting my next spell. I had no time to waste—I had to move fast for the payoff, so there was no time for amplification.

"No!" Zanaffar roared. "I, defeated by a mere sorceress?!"

Several tentacles writhed toward me. It was too late, since I already had my deathblow ready to go, but I wanted to get a comeback line in first.

"You've taken this *mere sorceress* too lightly, Zanaffar!" I shouted. "I hope you like your ribs ...*well done*!

"FIREBALL!"

FWOOM!

Zanaffar's midsection rumbled as tongues of flames shot out from his ears, nose, and mouth. He couldn't even scream as the fiery inferno devoured him from within.

As I fell to the ground nearby, exhausted, I watched the bastard burn. The acrid smell of cooked flesh singed my nostrils and burned my eyes.

Ahh . . . the smell of victory. It was less than appetizing, but still oddly sweet.

***

"Mmm." I slumped and sighed with relief. I held up both my hands and inspected them carefully; they looked and felt a million times better, thanks to Amelia's resurrection spell.

"You rock," I told her, glancing in her direction. She was in the middle of casting a recovery spell on Gourry's injured leg, but she still managed to nod a quick "You're welcome."

At the end of every major battle, it's the healers who save the day. Remember that the next time you form your adventuring party.

"Lina?" Gourry asked, then grunted in pain as Amelia poked his leg. "Can I ask you a question?"

Explanation time. "Shoot," I replied.

"How'd you kill Zanaffar?"

Right. Who called it?

I stretched out my arms and took a deep, satisfied breath. "Maybe you didn't see it," I explained. "I used my big spell to punch a hole in him, right? Then I just kept my arms in there and cast a fireball. It barbecued the sucker from the inside."

"Huh," Gourry replied, nodding vaguely. I was a little annoyed that he didn't seem impressed by my death-defying heroics. He thought a moment then frowned.

"Maybe I'm not thinking about this right," he added, "but wasn't that, like, really reckless?"

"*Very* reckless." Amelia finished tending to Gourry and got to her feet. "Actually," she said, gesturing to my hands, "Lina's hands were in worse shape than your leg, Gourry."

I shook my head, pushing my palms into my eyes. "Ugh," I groaned. "Don't remind me."

The fireball, you see, had gone off in my grip. So even with Zanaffar's inner body tissue providing protective padding, you can probably imagine what my hands had looked like when I'd pulled them from Zanaffar's incinerated carcass. I'd known the risks of the Ragna-Blade-plus-fireball strategy, of course, but that hadn't made torching my flesh any more fun.

Zelgadiss stood nearby, silently looking out at the horizon. I walked up to him and gingerly patted his shoulder.

"You gonna be okay?" I asked carefully. "Sorry we didn't end up getting the manuscript. You must be pretty bummed, huh?"

Zelgadiss shrugged. "Eh."

Eh?

I swallowed. "So, um . . . you're not angry because this ended up as a great big waste of time?"

"It wasn't a waste of time," he countered. "Think about it. We've proven the existence of the Claire Bible; all that's left now is to find it." His eyes caught mine, and I saw his pupils glitter with purpose. "And I *will* find it. You can count on that."

It was a surprisingly optimistic viewpoint, though it *was* a little weird, coming from him.

I thought Zelgadiss was the angsty one.

"Well," piped in Amelia. "I'm glad we can put this whole mess behind us now."

"Except for the fact that we dug ourselves into a deeper hole, you mean."

The others halted and shot me quizzical glances.

"*This* mess is done," I explained. "But what about all the huge loose ends?" They shook their heads, not quite getting it.

"Xelloss?" I offered. "The Claire Bible?"

"Oooooh."

Whatever. There would be plenty of time for all that later. I never backed down from a challenge—not then and not now.

As I stared off into the distance, I felt an iron resolve fill me. I was determined to face the next day and every day that followed with my middle finger raised high.

Hello, world—make way for Lina Inverse!

AFTERWORD

Kanzaka Hajime + **L**

Author: Hi, everyone! It's been awhile! Well, I finally got *Slayers Vol. 5: The Silver Beast* out the door!

L: Yeah, it *has* been awhile, hasn't it?

A: Ick! I know, I know, it's been too long. Y-you're not gonna sic **S** on me again, are you?

L: I just might. Why? You nervous?

A: Hmph! I'd like to see you try it! In case you don't recall, your popularity was way down in the last poll. You wouldn't dare harm your author and risk everybody hating you even more, would you?

THWAK!

L: Silence! That's enough of *that*!

A: Is that the best you've got? That punch didn't even hurt.

L: Guess you're quite the boxing manga-ka. But this *is* the Afterword, so I'll lay off. If anyone's gonna harm the author, it's gonna be Minion **S**. It's his turn.

A: Well, he doesn't have to make an appearance after every volume, does he?

L: Oh, this **S** is different from the earlier **S**. He's the same but different, know what I mean? But it doesn't matter; he's **S** either way.

A: I don't think you have any business calling him Minion **S**. After all, you're just a—

L: Hey! I totally outrank **S**. I have *way* more power than **S** does!

A: Well, that's true. There sure is a lot of foreshadowing in this "Afterword," huh?

L: Well, you all oughta know, you read it!

A: Guess it did.

L: You *guess*? You planned the whole thing in advance, didn't you?

A: Sorta. I knew I wanted characters to pop back into the story later, but beyond that, I didn't have too much planned out.

L: That's not planning! That's just putting ideas together piecemeal and writing them in, isn't it?

A: I dunno.

L: Oh, so you're gonna play dumb now. That's your game, huh? Anyway, to change the subject: the topic for this volume's contest will follow along with the author's current interests.

A: Ah, yes! Summer! Sun! Tasty barley tea! If it's gonna reflect my interests, then I think it oughta be called, "The Big Summer Horror Story Contest!"

L: Sounds morbid. Are you into necromancy now?

A: Like hell I am! What makes you say that?! By horror stories, I don't mean "This Really Happened" kinda stuff. Of course, real-life stories are fine, and so are urban legends, or even fables you totally make up yourself. You can also submit your own "Scary Movie Scene" as long as it's totally original, so no ripping-off of movies, TV shows, books, or anything else that's already out there.

L: Huh. I think I've cracked your code, Hajime Kanzaka! You just want material for your own writing, don't you?!

A: No, no, no! It's just personal interest, that's all.

L: If this is personal, then you're one sick dude.

A: At the author's discretion, winners will receive one of my ever-popular prizes, such as colored paper illustrations. And, also, I liked **L's** suggestion that, if the author REALLY likes a particular submission, then it should be added to the

Afterword of the next volume along with full credit given to the winning participant.

L: My question is, why'd you choose horror stories as your topic?

A: That goes back to when I read this foreign story called, "The Headless Horseman." I'd never heard of it until I picked it up and started reading it, so I had no idea what to expect. Anyway, I REALLY liked it! So, I figured, *Why not open up the field to more horror stories?* It seemed like a cool idea.

L: I get it. So you're scratching the itch, huh?

A: Oh, and another thing: "Stories that Seem Scary but Are Actually Really Funny" are fair game too.

L: Fine! Fine! So what's the deadline?

A: Well, since it's a summer contest, I thought using it as a kick-off to summer might work. But then again, making the deadline the day before we go to press on the next volume might be too soon. I could also keep the contest going 'til we get three similar but somehow unfamiliar facial drawings published. So, what I'm trying to tell you is, there's no set deadline.

L: Okay, so what was the point of this Afterword? You've decided nothing.

A: Well, nothing new there.

L: You got that right.

A: I like to roll with the punches. *Ow!* I don't mean *real* punches Okay, take care, everybody.

L: 'Til next time. Hopefully, we'll be back before long. Isn't that right, Mr. Author?

A: Ugh! Ow! Stop it! Yeah, yeah, sure. Goodbye, everybody.

L: (Don't say anything! Don't say anything!)

IN THE NEXT VOLUME...

Slayers

6

Vezendi's Shadow

"Come to Vezendi, or someone will die," warns Zuuma.
Looks like there's no choice for Lina, Amelia, Gourry, Zelgadiss, and Xelloss but to set off for Vezendi—where lesser demons, bandits, and anything else you can think of—are ready and willing to take them down. Since Zuuma will stop at nothing to seek his revenge on Lina and Gourry, they finally decide that now is the time to finish him off once and for all . . . but will their efforts alone be enough?

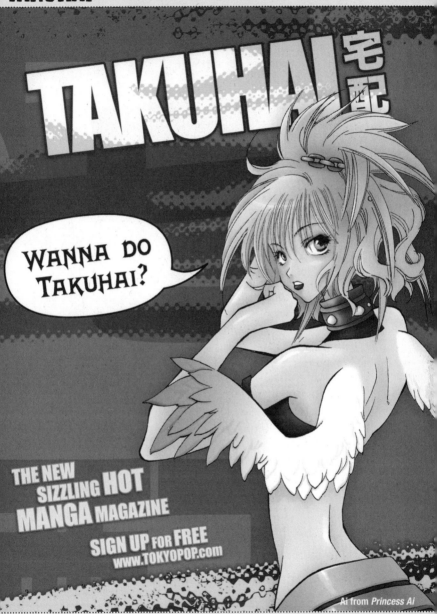

TOKYOPOP SHOP

Written by Keith Giffen, comic book pro and English language adapter of *Battle Royale* **and** *Battle Vixens.*

Join the misadventures of a group of particularly disturbing trick-or-treaters as they go about their macabre business on Halloween night. Blaming the apples they got from the first house of the evening for the bad candy they've been receiving all night, the kids plot revenge on the old bag who handed out the funky fruit. Riotously funny and always wickedly shocking— who doesn't *love* Halloween?

OT
OLDER TEEN
AGE 16+

BY REIKO MOMOCHI

CONFIDENTIAL CONFESSIONS

If you're looking for a happy, rosy, zit-free look at high school life, skip this manga. But if you're jonesing for a real-life view of what high school's truly like, *Confidential Confessions* offers a gritty, unflinching look at what really happens in those hallowed halls. Rape, sexual harassment, anorexia, cutting, suicide...no subject is too hardcore for *Confidential Confessions*. While you're at it, don't expect a happy ending.

~Julie Taylor, Sr. Editor

BY LEE SUN-HEE

NECK AND NECK

Competition can bring out the best or the worst in people...but in *Neck and Neck*, it does both! Dabin Choi and Shihu Myoung are both high school students, both children of mob bosses, and each is out to totally humiliate the other. Dabin and Shihu are very creative in their mutual tortures and there's more than a hint of romantic tension behind their attacks. This book's art may look somewhat shojo, but I found the story to be very accessible and very entertaining!

~Rob Tokar, Sr. Editor

BY AKI SHIMIZU

SUIKODEN III

I'm one of those people who likes to watch others play video games (I tend to run into walls and get stuck), so here comes the perfect manga for me! All the neat plot of a great RPG game, without any effort on my part! Aki Shimizu, creator of the delightful series *Qwan*, has done a lovely, lovely job of bringing the world of Suikoden to life. There are great creatures (Fighting ducks! Giant lizard people!), great character designs, and an engaging story full of conflict, drama and intrigue. I picked up one volume while I was eating lunch at my desk one day, and was totally hooked. I can't wait for the next one to come out!

~Lillian Diaz-Przybyl, Editor

BY TOW NAKAZAKI

ET CETERA

Meet Mingchao, an energetic girl from China who now travels the deserts of the old west. She dreams of becoming a star in Hollywood, eager for fame and fortune. She was given the Eto Gun—a magical weapon that fires bullets with properties of the 12 zodiac signs—as a keepsake from her grandfather before he died. On her journey to Hollywood, she meets a number of zany characters...some who want to help, and others who are after the power of the Eto Gun. Chock full of gun fights, train hijackings, collapsing mineshafts...this East-meets-wild-West tale has it all!

~Aaron Suhr, Sr. Editor

KAMICHAMA KARIN
BY KOGE-DONBO

Karin is an average girl...at best. She's not good at sports and gets terrible grades. On top of all that, her parents are dead and her beloved cat Shi-chan just died, too. She is miserable. But everything is about to change—little does Karin know that her mother's ring has the power to make her a goddess!

From the creator of *Pita-Ten* and *Digi-Charat!*

© Koge-Donbo.

KANPAI!
BY MAKI MURAKAMI

Yamada Shintaro is a monster guardian in training—his job is to protect the monsters from harm. But when he meets Nao, a girl from his middle school, he suddenly falls in love...with her neckline! Shintaro will go to any lengths to prevent disruption to her peaceful life—and preserve his choice view of her neck!

A wild and wonderful adventure from the creator of *Gravitation!*

© MAKI MURAKAMI.

MOBILE SUIT GUNDAM ÉCOLE DU CIEL
BY HARUHIKO MIKIMOTO

École du Ciel—where aspiring pilots train to become Top Gundam! Asuna, daughter of a brilliant professor, is a below-average student at École du Ciel. But the world is spiraling toward war, and Asuna is headed for a crash course in danger, battle, and most of all, love.

From the artist of the phenomenally successful *Macross* and *Baby Birth!*

© Haruhiko Mikimoto and Sostu Agency · Sunrise.